D1191834

BIRD ILLUSTRATORS

BIRD ILLUSTRATORS

SOME ARTISTS IN EARLY LITHOGRAPHY

BY

C. E. JACKSON

H. F. & G. WITHERBY LTD

First Published in 1975 by
H. F. & G. Witherby Ltd.
5 Plantain Place, Crosby Row
London S.E.1

© *C. E. Jackson 1975*

ISBN 0 85493 103 1
Made in Great Britain

Composed in Monotype Walbaum
and Printed by The Compton Press Ltd.
Compton Chamberlayne, Salisbury
Wiltshire

THE HOLDEN ARBORETUM
LIBRARY

6464

PREFACE

A NEW method of printing multiple copies of artists' drawings, known as lithography, was invented a few years before Queen Victoria's accession. It was used extensively throughout her long reign for the beautifully illustrated books which were a feature of the Victorian era. These illustrations were made by drawing on flat slabs of limestone and printing from the image deposited by the greasy ink or chalk of the drawing. The resulting black and white print, or lithograph, was then coloured by hand, using water-colour paints. Later, craftsmen discovered how to print from the stones with coloured inks and so eliminate the labour of colouring prints by hand. Hand-coloured lithographs and chromo-lithographs were favoured by bird-artists more than any other type of illustration during the period 1830 to 1900 when some of the finest bird books were printed.

This book tells the story of the use of lithography for bird book illustration. It commences with the adoption of the new process by Swainson, and then follows the careers of other bird-artists as they develop it for their own particular purpose and style. There is a description of the life and work of each bird-artist, resident in Britain, who used the medium. All the important bird books illustrated with lithographs and published in this country, have been reviewed. Books on falconry, domestic poultry and cage birds have been omitted, with the exception of one or two titles which included outstanding examples of an artist's work.

Limiting the scope of the book to include only those artists whose drawings were reproduced lithographically has resulted in the omission of such famous artists as Audubon (whose drawings were reproduced by aquatint engraving), Bewick the wood-engraver, and many others. It is hoped that a further volume will be published, making good these omissions and discussing the work of the bird-artists whose designs were reproduced by wood and metal engravings.

5

CONTENTS

ILLUSTRATIONS

Full captions to each plate are printed at the end of the text dealing with each artist.

Where a size of the bird is indicated on the plate, this should not be regarded as accurate, because some of the plates have been enlarged, and others reduced from the originals, to conform with the page size of this book.

ACKNOWLEDGEMENTS

MANY librarians have gone to a great deal of trouble in locating and supplying books for consultation. Among these I should particularly like to acknowledge the help I have received from Miss L. V. Paulin and the staff of the Hertfordshire County Library; R. Hughes, the Librarian of the Balfour Library, Zoology Department, Cambridge University who is custodian of original Gould and Swainson material; Dr David Snow and the staff of the Bird Room, also the staff of the Zoology Library, the British Museum (Natural History); the County Librarian of Bedfordshire and his staff. Their friendly cooperation was most encouraging.

Only two of the bird-artists in this book have been the subjects of full-scale biographies. I should like to draw attention to these valuable sources. The first to be published was A. H. Palmer's *The life of Joseph Wolf* (Longman 1895). It is particularly interesting because some of the material was supplied by Wolf himself. Edward Lear has been the subject of a number of studies, the most intensively researched being that by Mrs. V. Noakes, published by Collins in 1968. She has quoted a number of Lear's letters, hitherto unpublished, which reveal a great deal about Lear as a man and artist. Without these two sources in particular, my task would have been much harder.

I received many helpful suggestions and criticisms from my husband, Andrew B. Jackson. These were not always fully appreciated at the time, but I am pleased to acknowledge them here.

We take pleasure in acknowledging the gracious consent of F. W. Frohawk's wife, Mrs M. J. Frohawk, and his daughter Valeznia, Viscountess Bolingbroke, to our reproducing his plate of the Chatham Island Pigeon. Henrik Grönvold's daughter, Mrs Elsa Ayres, too, took an interest in the chapter relating to her father and generously gave her permission to use Grönvold's picture of the Red-tailed and Red-winged Guans. The plate by G. E. Lodge of the Falcon with Ptarmigan came from Thornton's *A Sporting Tour* published by Edward Arnold Ltd. We are pleased to acknowledge the publisher's permission to in-

11

ACKNOWLEDGEMENTS

clude this typical Lodge composition. Archibald Thorburn's Eagle Owl is reproduced by the courtesy of Lord Lilford and the Tryon Gallery, and our thanks are due to them for enabling us to include this example of the excellent chromolithographs done for Lord Lilford, the 4th Baron.

We apologise should we have failed to trace the true owners of any of those plates which may still be in copyright, but trust that sufficient recompense will be the renewed interest shown in them by their publication.

I should like to express my most sincere thanks to Dr Gwynne Vevers of the Zoological Society of London for his help in arranging the photography of plates reproduced from books in the Society's library, and to Mr R. A. Fish, the librarian there, for his kindness and encouragement during the preparation of this book. I am also indebted to Sir Samuel Cooke and Mr Colin Macpherson for making available to me the Edward Lear and Foster plates. The photographic work was undertaken by Mr A. C. Parker and I wish to thank him for the enthusiasm which he brought to his task and to record my admiration for his skill in overcoming the many problems involved in photographing the original plates.

Throughout each stage in preparing this book I received a great deal of encouragement and practical assistance from my publisher, Mr Antony Witherby to whom I am especially grateful.

THE BACKGROUND

THE first hand-coloured lithographic plate illustrating a bird was published in 1820 and the last one in 1936. In the intervening years many other bird illustrations were reproduced by copper-engraving, wood-engraving and colour printing processes, but the favourite method of illustrating bird-books was by hand-coloured lithographs. Authors and artists favoured this process because it was relatively easy to execute and the results were as close to the original water-colours as any printing process of that period allowed.

The method of publishing these bird-books differed in a number of ways from the way in which our books are published today. These important differences, if understood, enable us to appreciate more fully the bird-books published in the 19th century and help us to recognise the achievements of their authors, illustrators and printers.

For the author, finding a subject was a much easier business than nowadays when everything seems to have been said many times over. He could describe, for the first time, the many new species which were then being discovered as trade routes and new countries were opened up. Almost the whole of the avifauna of Australia was waiting to be discovered and described and much of the African avifauna was in the same virgin state. Ornithologists were still working out Linnaeus' ideas and trying to arrange the birds in family groups and discover the affinities between similar species from different parts of the world. No-one had published a book which dealt exclusively with one bird family. Edward Lear was to make this novel approach to the subject with a book of illustrations of members of the parrot family in 1830-32. Although books about our native birds had already been issued in the two preceding centuries, so many additional species were being added to our national list, and more information about their habits and distribution was coming to light, that constant revision of the records of British birds was necessary.

Having decided on his subject, the author's next consideration was to obtain sufficient material for his text and the illustrations. Living in London was not only a great advantage, but almost essential. The main collection of specimens was in the British Museum. Live models were available after 1826 when the Zoological Society of London was established and its gardens opened to the public a few years later. Membership of the Linnean, Royal and Zoological Societies was eminently desirable, not only for the prestige which it brought but also for the access to books, journals and specimens which it gave. Another advantage was meeting fellow-naturalists, and for an author who needed recommendations to wealthy patrons this was the easiest way to meet such people and seek introductions. Many of the wealthy land-owners of this period followed the fashion of establishing menageries in their grounds and were keen members of natural history societies. Frequently the wealthy patrons had both private menageries and museums of their own, with many new species and specimens bought by them and housed in the extensive grounds of their country properties. One such landowner might have the only parrot or owl of a certain species in the whole of the United Kingdom, and being acquainted with him was the first step to obtaining an invitation to visit the aviary in order to draw the bird and write a description of it.

There was no point in starting on the project unless sufficient copies could be sold to cover the costs of producing the book. About two hundred subscriptions were required for the book to be an economic success. Soliciting subscribers was the author's responsibility. He sometimes issued a prospectus, a sheet of paper folded once, the outside giving details of the proposed book, its title, author, contents, illustrations and the reputation of the artist. The inside of the sheet was used to extol the publication, its author, its scope and comprehensiveness and generally to convince prospective buyers that it promised to be an important publication they could not do without and which would, moreover, be of good value. Another practice to encourage subscribers was to advertise the book on the wrappers of someone else's book already in the process of being issued to readers of similar tastes and interests. These advertisements often carried a list of subscribers already committed to purchasing the parts as issued. The aim then, was to get "The Queen" at the head of the list (often by presenting her with a copy rather than by Her Majesty's actually paying for her own copy) followed by as many Dukes, Earls, etc. as possible, and so on down to plain Mr Smith at the tail end. Friends and fellow-authors invariably appeared in these lists, and authors who were members of the societies could count on fellow-members to swell the number of subscribers. These methods of canvassing prospective buyers in advance of publication no doubt led to the lengthy descriptive titles used by their authors and the very immodest, glowing terms in which they described their own work. No author today would dare say in his title that "The birds are most faithfully drawn from nature and beautifully coloured..." but a Victorian author desperate for subscribers had to be his own advertiser.

Large format 19th century bird-books were not published in a complete volume and sold to the public in book-shops. They were issued in parts, each containing five or more illustrations, accompanied by some letterpress, with a wrapper bearing the title and author's name, the number of the part and the date of its issue, and perhaps carrying some advertisement matter on the back. These fascicules, or parts, were issued at monthly or bi-monthly intervals, as a rule. When all the parts had been printed, the plates and text were re-arranged to group bird families together. This was necessary because the author usually made each part more attractive and interesting by including a number of different kinds of birds from several families. A contents list, introduction, and occasionally an index, were printed with the last part. After arranging the sheets, they were bound into one or more volumes by the person who had purchased the individual parts. Sometimes it was possible to purchase bound-up volumes when all the parts had been issued, but very often this was quite out of the question as only sufficient copies of the parts to satisfy subscribers had been printed. This, of course, gave the book an "exclusive" value and encouraged subscribers to place their orders early.

As the copies of the parts were printed, they had to be delivered to the subscribers. Authors who were their own publishers had to undertake this irksome task themselves. They found it time-consuming and uncongenial, since they had also to collect the subscription. Frequently, the subscribers got tired of the book long before the final part had been published, and if too many dropped out, the author had to start canvassing for replacement subscribers in order to avoid a financial loss. This also entailed reprinting earlier plates and text for the new subscribers, and often, by the time the last part had been issued, the author had no idea how many copies of each plate had been printed. Authors who left this work to a publisher or agent gained in time and avoided much vexation of spirit, but had to pay for their services and so reduced their profits.

Delivery of the parts would be easy when the subscribers and author were either resident in London, or visiting the capital regularly for attendance at society meetings. When scattered over a wide area, delivery must have presented a number of formidable problems. Most probably, many of the books in the early part of our period, went by coach, and very large, bulky parcels they must have made. Folio sized plates are approximately $22'' \times 16''$ and would be spoiled if folded or rolled. The railways would be the next carriers, and the last of the folio size parts, belonging to Mathews' *Birds of Norfolk and Lord Howe Islands* in 1936 most probably went via His Majesty's royal mail.

The authors and artists chose the royal folio or folio size for a number of reasons, mainly to do with the lithographs which embellished them. Edward Lear, who was his own artist and lithographer, was the first to choose this format, in 1830. He drew his parrots life-size and transferred them in the same natural size onto the lithographic stones, thus eliminating the difficulties which a reduction in scale causes and with which Swainson had had to contend. Artists dislike the reduction in size which a smaller page requires. Added to this, the lithographic process shows at its best in large, bold designs.

The author, having obtained an assured number of subscribers, decided on the format of the book, collected his material and written his text, now had to consider the illustrations. In the early days of lithographic bird illustration, the author, artist and lithographer were frequently one and the same person. Occasionally the author made the project a family concern with husband and wife, sometimes children, involved in producing the illustrated book. Later, when bird-artists had sufficient work to devote their whole time to illustrating birds, an author would commission a number of drawings and then either pay the artist to transfer them onto the stones, or employ a lithographer to do that part of the job. When the author employed an artist he would help with finding and making available specimens for the artist to do the sketches and drawings. If a monograph of a family were being published all the species they could find would be included. Avifaunas of different countries would need to be fully covered in the text, but common species need not be illustrated, and it was usual to select the rarest or new species only for illustrating.

In the early part of the century, the artist's task was merely to provide an outline of the bird, with its feather contours, much as a draughtsman would show the shape and design of some inanimate object. Careful delineation of the details of claws, position of nostrils on the beak, emargination of the feathers, etc. were essential details. Not until Lear painted more individual members of the species, giving them bird-characters, and then Wolf went a stage further and captured his birds in fleeting moments of life, did the artist begin to be a genuine bird-artist as opposed to a zoological draughtsman. It was the realisation of the new freedom which lithography gave the artist which helped make this transformation. Gradually the idea of making pictures took shape, with habitat scenes in the background and interesting additional sketches of nests, eggs, and immature birds in the progressive stages of their development, added to the foreground.

THE BACKGROUND

The new freedom in style in which the drawings could be done was an obvious attraction to the artists whose sketches were going to be copied by a lithographer. An artist preparing a drawing for an engraver to copy had had to bear in mind the limitations that the material, wood or metal, imposed on the engraver, for an engraver could not draw a curve with a sweeping movement of the hand, he had to hold the engraver or stylus still in one hand and move the whole metal plate with his other hand. A lithographer could draw a curve with almost the same ease as a person with a pencil, brush or chalk. Swainson the first of the mainstream of lithographic bird-book illustrators, did not grasp this basic difference. His feather details, instead of being scale-like, or a series of short sharp curves easy for a lithographer to copy, were continuous, longer, shallower lines more suitable to the engraver. Gradually, the greater freedom of line was exploited and less tight-wristed drawing is seen in the work of Mrs Gould, Hart, and Richter than in that of Swainson and Lear. Wolf was the first to achieve great freedom, largely because he was trained as a lithographer.

Another very interesting change in the style of the artists occurred during the course of this century. Wolf must take the credit for the new approach to painting birds. He was the first artist who made a successful full-time career of painting animals and birds, doing that and nothing else. He achieved this because he knew and loved the birds as wild, living, free creatures. The earlier artists had gone to the museums and copied specimens. Their pictures, or diagrams, show still birds perched on a branch or block, much as they saw them in the glass case in the museum. Wolf went out into the countryside and looked at the birds in their natural habitats. Throughout the 19th century, the illustrators divide themselves neatly into two camps, the museum men or zoological draughtsmen who worked from specimens, and the bird-artists like Wolf, Lodge and Thorburn who were bird-watchers as well as bird-painters. Their work is superior to that of the museum men.

Lithography was the last of the hand illustration processes to be invented, and it is also the only printing method whose inventor is know with certainty. Alois Senefelder was a Pole and worked in Prague in 1798 experimenting with stones and greasy ink. Having perfected his process he visited England in 1801 and demonstrated it in London. There was a certain amount of enthusiasm following this visit, but this waned. Charles Joseph Hullmandel (1789-1850) again demonstrated the process in 1818 in his book *Twenty-four Views of Italy* and the beauty of the illustrations once more raised a good deal of interest in lithography. Ackermann then published an English translation of Senefelder's *Complete Course of Lithography*, explaining how the process worked, and this was quickly followed by another book by Charles Hullmandel, *The Art of Drawing on Stone*, in 1824. Hullmandel was not only England's first successful lithographer, but he is important to us for the number of early lithographs of birds which he printed. He was interested in the process from an artistic point of view and not only owned presses for the reproduction of prints but he was a lithographer himself and did some fine lithographs of birds after other artists' drawings. It was to him that Lear turned for the printing of his lithographs, and then Gould used Hullmandel's presses for printing a good proportion of his three thousand plates. Until his death in 1850, Hullmandel's firm produced a high percentage of the litho-graphed bird-illustrations in books printed in England. He set a very high standard. Part of his success may be attributed to his having obtained very good quality stones from France.

Lithography is a planographic process, i.e. a method of surface printing where the image is on the same plane as the plate, in this case, a stone. Lithographic stones are almost pure limestone with the property of quick absorption of both water and grease. They range in colour from blue-grey to yellow, the colouring indicating the quality of the stone. The greyer stones are more uniformly receptive to grease, are harder, and more dense, thus producing a finer grain. Seen through a magnifying glass, a lithograph has the ground represented by a series of specks or dots—reproducing the porous surface and grain of the stone—the finer the stone, the smaller the specks. The process is based on the principle of the antipathy of grease to water. The lithographic stone has a natural affinity for grease so the image is drawn by the artist on the stone, in reverse (so that when the paper is pressed onto the surface face down, the image would transfer with the design the right way round) with greasy lithographic chalk or ink. This drawing will attract the oily ink used in printing. The rest of the stone is etched with a gum arabic and nitric solution. The acid opens the pores of the stone and allows both the gum and grease to enter. The gum arabic surrounds the greasy portions and repels water, and it also prevents the grease from spread-ing and blurring the image. In printing, the stone is dampened, the gum arabic repels the water and a film of printing ink adheres to the greasy drawing. The paper is pressed onto the face of the stone and the ink is trans-ferred to the paper.

A special press was necessary to cope with the heavy stone as it was difficult to apply even pressure over the whole surface of its flat bed. Hand-presses were used at first, the litho-machine presses not being introduced until the 1850s. Special paper was required owing to the amount of water used in the printing and special ink was also necessary. The greasy ink was made from lard, wax, and soap, to which were added shellac, venetian turpentine, carbonate of soda and paris black. Often, the resulting ink was browner or greyer than normal printer's ink, a factor which is used as an indication that the lithographic process was used.

Lithography may be recognised by the even colour of the ink, the wide range of tones between light and very dark and the lack of sharp crisp lines. Lithography has a very limited ability to give line so that subjects requiring broad effects, rather than minute detail are more satisfactorily reproduced. It is best used on large paper with bold designs. The use of folio-sized plates to illustrate bird-books was no mere whim on Lear's, and then Gould's part. The process of lithography influenced their choice. The fine bird-books of the 19th century were of folio format for the natural size of the birds depicted suited the medium best.

As a medium it quickly became popular with bird-artists because it lent itself to freedom of line. Engraving was a difficult craft and had to be executed by a skilled craftsman, but the artist could draw his own designs on the lithographic stone. Instead of using his pencil or brush, he used greasy chalk or ink. He had to work in reverse, which took some getting used to, but a little practice soon gave him command. If he could not achieve this, he used a transfer paper enabling him to draw the right way round. It was a distinct advantage to the artist to be able to draw his own designs on the stone and have the prints taken directly from it with no other craftsman or interpretive process coming between his design and the finished print which was virtually an exact reproduction or facsimile. The process was in vogue at the same period in which the English water-colour artists were flourishing. The basic outline of their sketches could be reproduced accurately and the washes put on by hand afterwards so that the finished prints were close facsimiles of the originals. The bird-plates done in this manner were thus the nearest thing to having original water-colour drawings in books which could be devised. A veritable army of hand-painters of the prints was employed to do the colouring, but as labour was cheap, it was possible to produce the book relatively cheaply.

The softer tones of lithography were thought to suit bird illustration better than the harsher lines of copper and steel engravings. The last ornithological work of note to contain metal-engraved illustrations was Selby's *Parrots* of 1843. Monochrome wood-engravings were still popular in the 1840s and hand-coloured wood-engravings continued to appear until mid-century when colour-printed wood-engravings or chromo-xylographs superseded them. Hand-coloured lithographs were still popular for bird-prints, despite the competition not only from chromo-xylography but also from chromolitho-graphy which was developed in the early 1850s.

The first English bird book to have lithographs was Swainson's *Zoological illustrations* 1820-23, the lithography being done by Swainson himself. The next title was by an American author and was a book about the birds of Java. Dr Thomas Horsfield's *Zoological researches in Java and the neighbouring islands* was issued in eight parts, each with four coloured plates. Dr Horsfield had collected his animals, birds and plants whilst living in Java 1811-17 when the island was under British rule. When his account of the zoology of the island was completed in 1824 he had described and figured thirty three species among the the thirty-six birds shown on the plates, among them twenty new eastern birds. A number of the birds had been drawn by Auguste Pelletier, and he and Hullmandel transferred the designs onto the stones. The plates were then coloured under Pelletier's superintendance. This early work truly reflects the period in which it was produced, for some of the plates in the book were copper-engravings after John Curtis' designs and it was decided that the illustrations of the new genera could not be shown sufficiently clearly by lithography, so they were shown in great detail on the engraved plates. These early lithographs have a certain stiffness, but are competently executed.

After this tentative beginning, the next book had ninety plates of birds, all lithographs. This was J. E. Gray and Thomas Hardwicke's *Illustrations of Indian Zoology*, 1830-34. Major-General Hardwicke's collection of Indian birds was made when he served in the military service of the Honourable East Indian Company. He had employed a native artist to draw the birds, and from these water-colour drawings and other specimens in the British Museum, Benjamin Waterhouse Hawkins drew the images on the stones. The number of printers employed shows the increasing interest being taken in lithography and reflects the success which attended the early experiments in this medium. More firms were learning to exploit the growing demand for colour-illustrated books. Hullmandel printed only one of the plates for *Illustrations of Indian Zoology*, William Day, Graf & Soret, and Engelmann & Co., contributing the remainder.

Godefroi Engelmann was a leading Parisian lithographer who had opened a business in London in 1827. Auguste Graf was in charge of this end of the business but it did not pay and closed down in 1830. Graf & Soret were in business c1830–1840 and they also did some plates for Gray and Hardwicke. William Day (1797–1845), the last contributor, had been in the London Directory since 1829 as a "lithographic printer and press manufacturer".

His name was to reappear many times during the next eighty years in bird-book imprints in the varying firm of W. Day, Day & Haghe, Day & Son, and Vincent Brooks, Day & Son.

Another firm of lithographers which printed many bird illustrations was that of M & N Hanhart. Michael Hanhart began work in Engelmann's firm, then with his two sons established his own business in Charlotte Street, London, c1830. This flourished for sixty years, doing both hand-coloured lithography and chromolithography. Birds prints were lithographed by the Hanharts for Dresser's *Birds of Europe, Meropidae* and *Coraciidae*; for Seebohm's *Geographical distribution of the Charadriidae*; for Shelley's *Nectariniidae* and a number of books written by P. L. Sclater.

Besides, Hullmandel, the printers T. Walter & Cohen were employed by Gould. This firm produced hand-coloured lithographs in the latter half of the 19th century when other firms were more interested in printing in colour. They worked on Gould's *Birds of Asia, Birds of Australia*, and his *Monograph of the Trochilidae*, also on Dresser's *Birds of Europe*, Rowley's *Ornithological Miscellany* and Hume's *Game birds of India*.

The only other firm to produce high-class hand-coloured lithographs of birds was Mintern Brothers. They were still flourishing in the 20th century, and producing the last few hand-coloured lithographs, but they also printed very good chromolithographs. They were the sole printers employed by the British Museum for their *Catalogue of Birds*, whose first thirteen volumes had hand-coloured lithographs and whose last fourteen volumes had chromo-lithographs and were issued over the twenty-four year period 1874–98. They worked on the hand-coloured illustrations for Salvin & Godman's *Biologia Centrali-Americana* 1879–1904 with Hanhart, on Sharpe's two monographs of the 1890s the *Paradiseidae* and *Hirundinidae*, and Seebohm's *Monograph of the Turdidae* 1888–1902.

Ever since printing had been invented in the last quarter of the 15th century, there had been a search for a method of good colour printing. Hullmandel, who had printed so many prints in monochrome, was the earliest exponent of printing in colour with lithography. Engelmann, who had employed Hullmandel at one stage, had patented a process he called chromo-lithography in France in 1837. Engelmann died two years later. Hullmandel did not exactly copy the method described by Engelmann in his *Manuel en couleurs* published in 1835, but developed another, similar idea, which he called lithotint. The word was chosen as a companion for aquatint and mezzo-tint. The process was described as "A new effect of light and shadow uniting a brush or stump drawing, or both combined, produced on paper, being an impression from stone...". It was, in effect, like an aquatint from stone.

Lithotint is an intermediate stage between monochromatic lithography and colour lithography or chromolithography. It consists of using several neutral tints, scraped down for the white highlights. It was most useful for reproducing chalk and wash drawings. Hullmandel, after much experimenting printed in two colours in 1836 in a book written by his friend Harding. Two years later, in Frank Howard's *Colour as a Means of Art* he tried partial printing in colours, but over-loaded the plates by hand-colouring, so defeating his purpose in demonstrating his new method of colour-printing. In 1839 he had more success, when he used four graduated transparent lithographic tints as well as black for the illustrations in Thomas Shotter Boys' *Picturesque Architecture in Paris*. These were lithotints rather than flat opaque colours and imitated Boys' wash drawings on tinted paper.

Two bird books were printed by Hullmandel's firm, Hullmandel & Walton, using his patent lithotint. They were George Robert Gray's *Genera of Birds* in three royal octavo volumes with 360 plates of which 185 were coloured, and G. R. Gray and R. B. Sharpe's commentary on the birds seen and collected on the *Erebus and Terror voyage* which had 17 coloured plates depicting birds. These volumes were published between 1837 and 1849. The delicate shades and tints are very beautiful.

After this, Hullmandel continued experimenting until his death in 1850. He did not live to see his firm's exhibition of specimens of his lithotint work at the Great Exhibition of 1851, but to him belongs the credit of producing a graduated tint, the use of white for highlights, and the use of liquid ink on the stone with a brush.

Many of the lithographs of the 1840s and early 1850s, in the numerous books illustrated by this process, have a modicum of printed tones, or tints, the rest of the colour having been applied by hand, just as the earlier aquatints had been finished by hand in water-colours. The next step, that from lithotint to the full chromolithograph, is an important one, for it involved colour separation. The grey foundation plate is used to give the tone range, but on top of that the colour is laid on by superimposition, from a number of separate stones, to give the desired hues.

For colour lithographic work, a separate stone was drawn for each colour. The stones were then printed separately in the appropriate colour in the printing machine. Often six or even more stones were used for different colours. Sometimes as many as twenty stones, besides the outline drawn on another stone as a key, were used for particularly rich effects. Each stone carried the design for one colour only and the paper was passed from stone to stone. Special art paper was no longer required. Good registration, i.e. the exact alignment of position of each successive printing on the paper from the series of colour stones, was absolutely essential, the success of the finished print depending on it.

The process is distinguished by deep, rich colours, and delicate tints being possible, with every shade between. The colours are bold, with strong contrasts, the process showing at its best when flat colours and gold are used.

The majority of the chromolithographs of the 1830s and 1840s were the black and tint kind, with salmon or lemon ground being a distinguishing feature of this period. The first really successful full chromolithographic book illustrations appeared in 1836 in Owen Jones' *Plans, elevations, sections and details of the Alhambra*. Each of these plates was prepared by colour application from six or seven stones.

Not until the 1850s was the process used very much for book work. Wolf was the first bird-artist to use the new medium. He used it in 1853, and then again in 1854, for some small bird-pictures illustrating poems. The British Museum *Catalogue of Birds* changed from hand-coloured lithographs to chromolithographs in volume XIV in 1888 but this is the only really large number of chromolithographs to be produced in one title except Lord Lilford's *Coloured figures* of 1885–97. Although Lord Lilford's book is a very fine piece of book production, it still did not serve to make chromolithography more popular than the hand-coloured lithographs.

Printing in colour was expensive. All the illustrations of bird books produced by this method had octavo size plates, or smaller format. This meant that the birds could not be shown life-size and had to be drawn to a reduced scale. The artists reverted to the practice of the engravers and placed a note at the foot of the plate stating the amount of reduction in size for each bird depicted.

There were very few chromolithographic printers of bird illustrations in this country. The Hanharts did some good work for Wolf's *Poets of the Woods*, 26 plates for Lord Lilford and some work in *Ibis* from 1859 onwards. Their early work employed flat tints only, then about 1850 they progressed to a black key stone with three colours added. In the plates for Lord Lilford they used full chromolithography where the colours formed the pictures themselves. They also used full lithographic colours in Wolf's *Feathered favourites* of 1854.

In Lord Lilford's opinion, the best chromolithographic printers were Greve of Berlin. This firm did 263 of his 421 chromolithographs for *Coloured figures*. He also employed the Chromo-Litho Art Studio to execute 44 plates and two other English firms contributed a few plates each; Judd & Co 12 plates; West, Newman & Co, 3 plates.

If these firms and their staff of lithographers and colourers had not been so competent and capable of producing prints of such excellent quality, they would never have lasted as long as they did. There was so much competition from other methods of reproduction. Photography finally superseded the hand lithographic processes at the turn of the century, for it could do the job so much more cheaply and quickly at a time when there was a demand for multiple copies of illustrated instructive nature books for the masses. The days of printing 200–250 copies in one edition only, for wealthy patrons, were past. With them went the period which can be considered the finest and best in coloured bird-book illustration.

Though we have tried in this book to give the reader some idea of the beautiful illustrations in the bird books of a century ago, we have had to use modern methods of reproducing these illustrations for this book. Inevitably, the illustrations have undergone a change as another method of reproducing them has been used. It is now impossible to issue a book of this kind with hand-coloured lithographs and chromolithographs, even as examples to show exactly what they looked like. Not only would the cost be prohibitive, but there are hardly any craftsmen capable of doing the work. The illustrations here reproduced were done by photolithography and are as near the originals as we can manage today. Some of the freshness and charm of the originals has been lost, but we hope that they are of sufficient quality to whet the reader's appetite and encourage him to seek out copies of the originals and enjoy looking at the illustrations for himself.

WILLIAM SWAINSON

1789-1855

WILLIAM SWAINSON was a versatile man. Though he was an all-round naturalist in the tradition of the 18th century, he was, nevertheless, first and foremost an ornithologist. He was also a great and enthusiastic traveller. Many regard him as one of the best zoological artists of his time, and he used his talent to illustrate many books. His earlier work was illustrated with copper-, steel-, and wood-engravings, but when lithography was becoming fashionable he quickly saw the advantages of using this method. For the first time he was able to draw the design and to execute it for the printing machine himself by preparing his own plate, so excluding the craftsmen who had always previously come between him and the finished print. He learnt the art, or craft, of lithography when he was thirty and produced some of the first bird books to be illustrated with hand-coloured lithographs.

He had always been an adventurous kind of man. From his earliest days when he spent most of his time out of doors collecting butterflies, shells, etc., he had had a great longing to travel abroad where no naturalist had been, in order to collect more exotic creatures. His father had formed a sizeable collection of British insects and shells in his home at Liverpool, which stimulated young William's interest. Soon, he became so knowledgeable that the authorities of the Liverpool Museum asked him to draw up *Instructions for collecting and preserving subjects of natural history*. A pamphlet of this title was printed privately in 1808.

Swainson's father was a collector of customs at Liverpool. When William was fourteen he was appointed a junior clerk in the same occupation. Perhaps the sight of the ships docking with their cargoes and sailing away again to far-distant ports made William even more determined to travel. His father obtained a post for him in the commissariat in order to give him a chance to

25

satisfy his amibition. In the spring of 1807 he went to Malta. After a short stay there, he crossed to Sicily, which was to be his base for the next eight years. Whilst with the English army garrisoning that island, he spent his leisure time collecting insects, plants, shells and fishes, and made many drawings of natural history objects. He also visited Morea, Naples, Tuscany, and was appointed chief of commissariat staff in Genoa. He was attracted to Greece and obtained leave of absence to go there. On the conclusion of peace in 1815, he returned to England, bringing his collections with him. He retired on half-pay as assistant commissary-general so that he could devote himself to the study of natural history and the writing up of his collections. His income was supplemented from time to time with the proceeds from the books and articles which he wrote.

Still wanting to see more of the world, Swainson decided to join Henry Koster when that explorer set off on his second journey to Brazil in the autumn of 1816. They arrived at Pernambuco safely, but because Brazil was in the throes of a revolution, Swainson could not penetrate into the interior of the country. He soon found this to be less of a disappointment than he originally thought, since he amassed such a large collection of birds and plants in the neighbourhood of Olinda, the Rio de Janeiro and the Rio San Francisco that he had sufficient material to keep him busy for many years to come. He took ship for Liverpool, where he arrived in 1818, and published a short account of his journey in the *Edinburgh Philosophical Journal* and then settled down to work on a written account of the specimens he had brought back with him.

Sir Joseph Banks recommended him for the honour of becoming a Fellow of the Royal Society in 1820. He had already been elected Fellow of the Linnean Society in 1816 before leaving for Brazil. He was well-known to the scientists of the day and corresponded with many of them. One of his friends was Dr William Elford Leach, an assistant keeper at the Natural History Department of the British Museum. Dr Leach had issued a *Zoological Miscellany* periodically, with a short account of new species which had been discovered. This had been illustrated with hand-coloured copper-engravings and included twenty-nine bird species over the period 1814–17. When Swainson was worrying about the expense involved in producing an illustrated account of new species, following the pattern of the *Zoological Miscellany*, Dr Leach suggested that he should learn to lithograph his own drawings and encouraged him to experiment with, and practise, the new process. Swainson soon succeeded in producing sufficiently good and accurate outlines of the subjects suitable for colouring by hand. In 1820 the first series of his octavo *Zoological illustrations* commenced publication. Swainson took upon himself the

W. Swainson

AZURE KINGFISHER

Alcedo azurea

whole expense and management of this work, so that he had to oversee the printing and hand-colouring of the plates himself. He had been publishing another work, *Exotic conchology* when the *Zoological illustrations* first came out but soon found that the uncertainty which then attended the lithographic process forced him to abandon *Exotic conchology* for the time being, remove to London, and devote the next three years entirely to the production of the monthly parts of *Zoological illustrations*. Because printing from lithographic stones was still in its infancy, Swainson found that his stones were frequently spoilt in the press and that he was obliged to draw the same subject twice, even three times on occasion, before the printers produced a good impression. He obviously suffered much from the teething troubles attending the new invention.

The parts of *Zoological illustrations* were eventually bound into three volumes and included one hundred and eighty-two of Swainson's autolithographs. These were accompanied by a description of the species and genera and included many new species and names. Of the autolithographs in this series, there were seventy plates of birds. The plates depicted either new or very rare species, the animals or birds being shown without any background. Usually a single bird was shown, though occasionally there was a pair. No attempt was made at representations of juveniles, eggs or nests, or states of alternative plumage. These refinements were not to be added until much later in the nineteenth century. The birds were accurately figured and the colouring good. Swainson's lithographic bird figures were done in the same style as the engraved figures which had appeared in other books by him. He drew with the lithographic chalk or ink exactly as he had prepared the drawings for an engraver to copy, with the same fine-lined details and straight or only slightly curved, strokes required for successful copper-engraving. He seems not to have fully realised the advantages of freedom of line and tone which the new process offered.

A second series of *Zoological illustrations* followed in 1829–33. Of the one hundred and thirty-six autolithographs forty-seven plates were of birds. Swainson added a scenic background to a few of these plates. He was a most accurate observer and artist. Only one plate in these volumes can be criticised with regard to a serious defect in the attitude of a bird. On the plate showing an Indian wren warbler, *Prinia familiaris*, (opposite page 97 in Series ii volume iii) the bird is placed on a branch, with its feet and legs in an impossible position—though one has to look twice to be convinced of this curious error.

Apart from the work involved in his own publications, Swainson undertook to do the designs for the birds in Sir John Richardson's account of the *Fauna Boreali-Americana*. Swainson and Richardson divided the work of describing the avifauna of the British American fur countries between them. Richardson had accompanied Sir John Franklin as surgeon and naturalist on Franklin's two land expeditions and had spent seven summers and five winters collecting in this part of America north of the 48th parallel. Richardson wrote about the habits of the two hundred and thirty-eight species, whilst Swainson did the arranging and naming of the birds. The monograph of the birds of the expedition was published in 1831, and included forty-nine hand-coloured lithographs by Swainson. The birds on these plates were scientifically accurate, though rather stiff, portraits. The figures were perched on a rock or a branch, with no background. When it came to preparing detailed diagrams of the heads of the species, wood-engravings were used—a recognition of the limited value of lithography as an illustration process. Lithography was to be used at a later date for detailed diagrams of the gut and some external features of birds, but it was not completely successful. The government gave a grant of £1000 towards the cost of printing the plates for this record of North American fauna, making this the first natural history work to be subsidised by the British government.

In 1834 the results of Swainson's study of the birds which he had brought back from Brazil some sixteen years before were first published. Over the next two years he issued seven parts of his *Ornithological Drawings* of the rarer and most interesting items in his collection. This had seventy-eight coloured autolithographs, but Swainson left it without a title-page, an index, or any text—as though he had quite lost interest in it by this time, having had so much other work for other people on hand. A new edition was issued in 1841 under a different title, *A Selection of the birds of Brazil and Mexico*, but this was also a half-hearted affair since for text it merely had a four-page list of the plates giving the English and scientific names of the seventy-eight species figured, these having been added by the publisher Henry Bohn after Swainson had left England. Only one hundred and seventy-five copies were printed and Swainson refused to sell any, except to those who subscribed originally for the parts. The book is small in size, has one bird or a pair of the same species on one plate, with a few branches and leaves. Swainson is still using a fine-line treatment with continuous lines used for the details of the feathers, unlike the curving scale-like treatment of later lithographers. The birds are life-like and quite lively.

Swainson's personal life had not been free from trouble. In 1825 he had married the only daughter of John Parkes of Warwick, and lived for a while with his in-laws. The following year his father died, leaving him an annuity of £200, but that ceased abruptly soon after, so that Swainson was forced to become a professional writer often working for others and delaying the work on the Brazilian birds. In 1828 he met Audubon and entertained him at his home near London. He must have been short of money, because after a trip to Paris with Audubon in September 1828, he borrowed £80 from the American. He then quarrelled with Audubon over a proposal to help him write *Ornithological Biography*, a text to complement Audubon's *Birds of America*. Audubon wanted Swainson's help mainly because his own English was not very good, his native language being French. Swainson was not prepared to give this aid unless his name appeared on the title-page. Also, Swainson demanded twelve guineas for each sheet of sixteen pages, and a further payment for proof correction. He also rejected Audubon's suggestion that he and his wife board with the Swainsons whilst writing the book, though both Mr and Mrs Audubon had stayed with the Swainsons for a very happy few days only a short while before this. So, Audubon turned to MacGillivray for assistance with his writing of *Ornithological Biography* and got it done by him at two guineas per sheet of sixteen pages. Despite this squabble, Audubon spoke highly of Swainson in *Ornithological Biography*, even dedicating a bird to Swainson by naming it Swainson's warbler. To give Swainson his due, he joined in a spirited defence of Audubon when the latter was unjustifiably attacked in an article written by the eccentric Charles Waterton who gave a completely erroneous account of the quarrel between Audubon and Swainson in *Loudon's Magazine* in May 1833. The trouble, basically, was that Swainson had some rather odd ideas about the classification of birds. He had become over-enthusiastic with regard to a strange theory put forward by a scientist called W. S. MacLeay, whose ideas were not accepted by many other scientists. Unfortunately, Swainson's obsession with this theory was to lead him to a point where his authority and credibility as an ornithologist were destroyed. Recognising this unpleasant truth almost certainly had a great deal to do with Swainson's decision to leave this country some years later.

Another sad episode occurred in 1835 with the death of his wife, leaving him with five children to bring up. Two years later, he lost half his fortune by the failure of two Mexican mines. He was to make up for this with other investments, but it was a blow at the time.

Meanwhile, Swainson was busily employed editing the eleven volumes of Lardner's Cabinet Cyclopaedia relating to natural history (1834–40) and in writing several volumes for Sir William Jardine's Naturalist's Library, among other literary pursuits. He was not happy, however, and felt further disgruntled when he failed to obtain a post he wanted at the British Museum. He decided to emigrate to New Zealand in 1840, accompanied by his second wife and their family, and ceased publishing works of natural history. He might well have been discouraged from writing further texts since he had the misfortune to lose a large portion of his collections due to the unseaworthy ship in which they sailed.

On reaching New Zealand he discovered that the glowing reports he had received concerning the new colony had been greatly exaggerated. He showed great courage in face of many difficulties and established himself on a farm. He also tended several plants he had brought with him from South America. These had been collected whilst his ship was being refitted at Rio de Janeiro. He hoped that these plants would flourish in the climate of New Zealand. No doubt he enjoyed discovering the new fauna and flora of that country, but unfortunately he did not publish any natural history descriptions in New Zealand. (A work on forestry in the colony often attributed to him was written by another immigrant of the same name, who arrived in New Zealand by way of Tasmania about the same time. His namesake (1809–1883) was later to become the first attorney-general of New Zealand). He died at Fern Grove, River Hutt, on 7th December 1855. Four sons of his first marriage and his wife and three daughters of the second marriage survived him.

In the Balfour Library, at the University of Cambridge, there is a portfolio of Swainson's sketches in pencil and water-colours for *Zoological Illustrations*, and some other drawings done at a later date. From these, it is evident that he was still drawing whilst in New Zealand. A note in his handwriting appears at the foot of a pencil sketch of the southern brown parrot *"Centrouros Australis"* which says, "Tongue added in New Zealand 1845 WS". On other sketches he has specified that the drawing was from a bird "in my own collection" or "altered from Edwards' drawing". He altered George Edwards' carinated toucan for his own figure of *Ramphastos carinatus*. So, even though busy with his farm, he maintained his interest in birds and continued to draw them.

Some years before leaving for New Zealand it would appear that Swainson had executed a dozen lithographs for a projected work on the birds of China by G. R. Gray. A year before his own death, Gray, who was then in charge of birds at the British Museum, decided to issue these few plates, with a short account of each of the species depicted, though no further work had been done on the book. This *Fasciculus of the birds of China* was published in 1871. The plates were both drawn and lithographed by Swainson, one of them being signed and dated "W. S. 11.30". The figures are less stiff than some others by him and there are a few trees and some ground work, all coloured. One figure is shown on each page. This is a charming fascicule, the plates being beautifully coloured and drawn, and it is a pity that further parts were not issued.

Swainson worked from specimens, not living birds. He was one of the best ornithological draughtsmen of his time. His experiments with lithography suffered from the influence of the engravers and the difficulties inherent in the early use of any new invention. Nevertheless, his birds are scientifically accurate and his portraits are true representations of their species. He demonstrated that lithography could be used successfully for bird-book illustrations. It was left to others to exploit the new medium more fully.

Books illustrated with lithographs by Swainson

GRAY, G. R. A Fasciculus of the birds of China 1871 12 plates hand-col. autolithogs.

RICHARDSON, SIR J. & SWAINSON, W. Fauna Boreali-Americana, or the zoology of the northern parts of British America, containing descriptions of the objects of natural history collected in the late northern land expeditions under the command of Cpt. Sir John Franklin: volume 2 Birds 1831 Plates 23–73 Artist 49 hand-col. lithogs.

SWAINSON, W. Zoological illustrations or original figures and descriptions of new, rare or otherwise interesting animals, selected chiefly from the classes of ornithology, entomology and conchology. 1820–23 3 vols. 182 plates (vol. I 24; vol. II 20; vol. III 26) = 70 hand-col. autolithogs of birds.
2nd series 1829–33 3 vols. 136 plates (vol. I 24; vol. II 15; vol. III 8) = 47 hand-col. autolithogs of birds.

SWAINSON, W. Ornithological drawings, being figures of the rarer and most interesting birds of Brazil. Series II Birds of Brazil 1834–36 78 plates hand-col. autolithogs.
2nd ed with new title A Selection of the birds of Brazil and Mexico 1841 78 plates hand-col. autolithogs.

Caption to Plate facing page 26

Swainson's Azure Kingfisher (*Alcedo azurea* from Zoological Illustrations 1st series 1820, vol. 1. Pl. 26) was autolithographed and hand-coloured for the first bird-book printed in Britain illustrated by lithography.

EDWARD LEAR

1812–1888

A WRITER of amusing nonsense verse but a melancholy man, admired by many friends though often lonely, with patrons among the rich men of England yet always struggling against poverty, this strange, genius of a man first made his name as the drawer and painter of highly individual members of the parrot family. Even so, his success as a bird-artist was cut short by the strain on his eye-sight which zoological draughtsmanship imposed. Only for a few years at the beginning of his career was Edward Lear able to draw and lithograph birds. It is remarkable that he achieved this, for he had no art training, nor scientific instruction, only the guidance of an elder sister who taught him to draw and paint birds, flowers and butterflies.

Edward Lear was the youngest of the twenty-one children born to stock-broker Jeremiah Lear and his wife Ann. They lived in a big house at Highgate with many servants and a fleet of twelve carriages. In 1825 financial disaster put the father in a debtor's prison, the house had to be let and the family split up. Edward's mother courageously set about paying off the debts so as to release her husband from gaol, but in so doing she neglected her many children. Anne, his elder sister by some twenty-one years, looked after Edward, who needed special care and attention for he was an extremely sensitive child and suffered from epileptic fits.

Many years later, when recalling these days, Lear wrote that by the time he was fifteen he was already trying to earn a living. "I began to draw, for bread and cheese about 1827 but only did uncommon queer shop-sketches—selling them for prices varying from 9d to four shillings; colouring prints, fans; awhile making morbid disease drawings, for hospitals and certain doctors of physic."

About two years after this, Lear must have been drawing birds to some

Edward Lear

RED-CAPPED PARAKEET
Platycercus pileatus

purpose and experimenting with lithography. Unfortunately, he destroyed his journals of these early years, so how he came to work in this manner is unknown. The first bird drawn by him which formed a book illustration is most probably the wood-engraving of a blue and yellow macaw in E. T. Bennett's book about the Zoological Gardens, which had been opened to the public in 1828, entitled *The Gardens of the Zoological Society delineated*. This was published in 1830 when Edward Lear was eighteen, and the vignette carried his monogram.

Two years earlier, Lear had come into contact with Selby. Prideaux John Selby was then publishing his *Illustrations of British Birds*, a beautiful book of hand-coloured copper-engravings. These life-size portraits were lively figures and Selby owed some of his technique to lessons he had had in Edinburgh in 1826 from Audubon the American bird painter. Selby's work was overshadowed by that of Audubon, but his plates are some of the best figures of British birds that have ever been published and Lear's contact with Selby resulted in his being able to produce more lively portraits of birds. Several plates in the later volumes of Jardine and Selby's *Illustrations of Ornithology* bear Lear's monogram.

Lear's attempts to reproduce his own designs by lithography date from 1830. He was planning to produce a series of portraits of the parrot family, hoping to draw all the species then known and issue a book, in fourteen folio parts, called *Illustrations of the family of Psittacidae or Parrots*. The first two parts were issued in November 1830 and were received by the public with general approval. Two members of the Linnean Society, E. T. Bennett and N. A. Vigors, recommended that Lear become an Associate of the Linnean Society, and he was admitted the day following the publication of the first two parts of his *Parrots*.

To portray all the members of one family of birds was a new idea. Hitherto authors had concentrated on birds of a specific region, or on broader groups, such as song-birds. Lear soon found that the parrots in the Zoological Gardens where he sketched were not complete representatives of their family. He borrowed parrots in the collections of Lady Mountcharles, Lord Stanley the President of both the Zoological and Linnean Societies, Mr Leadbeater who traded in bird skins and in 1851 had a cockatoo named after him (*Kakatoe leadbeateri*, the Pink Cockatoo), N. A. Vigors, Secretary of the Zoological Society, and John Gould at this time taxidermist to the society and collector of bird-skins on his own account.

Lear had been given permission, at a meeting of the Zoological Society on 16th June 1830, to make drawings from the parrots in the gardens in

Regent's Park, just a short walk from his home in Chester Terrace. He sat in the parrot house among the noisy, screeching birds, day after day, making pencil sketches and measuring the parrots whilst a keeper held them. Members of the public found the sight of Lear at work as intriguing as viewing the other inmates of the parrot house, to his great embarrassment. Sometimes he repaid their curiosity by making lightning cartoon sketches of their faces in the margins of his drawing-paper.

Having made copious notes and many pencil sketches of each species, Lear then drew his designs, in reverse, on lithographic stones with greasy chalk. He carried the heavy stones to Great Marlborough Street where Charles Hullmandel printed some copies from them in his workshop. Lear would then make any necessary adjustments or alterations to his drawings so that Hullmandel could print off sufficient copies for Lear to have coloured by hand and sent to his subscribers. Lear was his own publisher and had the oversight of the production of the prints as well as their distribution. This was a remarkable undertaking for a youth of eighteen.

Throughout the whole of 1831 he was busy with the drawings for his parrot book. When writing to a friend in October, he doubted his being able to offer that friend anywhere comfortable to sit down should he choose to visit him ". . . seeing,that of the six chairs I possess 5 are at present occupied with lithographic prints—the whole of my exalted and delightful tenement in fact overflows with them & for the last 12 months I have so moved— thought—looked at,—& existed among parrots—that should any transmigration take place at my decease I am sure my soul would be uncomfortable in anything but one of the Psittacidae".

As each part was completed to Lear's satisfaction, and he had very high standards, they were delivered to his one hundred and seventy-five subscribers. After receiving Part IX of his copy of the *Parrots*, one of the subscribers, William Swainson, wrote Lear a most appreciative and encouraging letter. Swainson thought that Lear's red and yellow macaw was more faithfully and realistically executed than any other bird-figure painted by either the great French artist Barraband, or by Audubon. Swainson also reviewed Lear's book favourably.

Despite all the praise, however, Lear abandoned his parrots after Part XII, issued in the spring of 1832. He wrote to Sir William Jardine, then publishing the Naturalist's Library volumes, that he had originally intended portraying all the parrots "but I stopped in time, neither will there be (from me) any letterpress." The work had achieved what Lear had required of it, recognition of his talents and employment for him for some time to come.

Quite what he meant by saying he had stopped in time is not known. One can speculate that the reason may have been that he did not make any profit from the publication. In the same letter to Sir William Jardine, dated 23.1.34, he says that the project "in the matter of money occasionally caused loss". John Gould bought up the remainder of his stock, with a view to completing the work, but he never did so.

The collection of forty-two hand-coloured lithographs was the first book of lithographed birds published in England on this scale. (Swainson had chosen octavo size for his books.) Gould was to follow Lear's example and produce all his bird-books in this format and by this method. Lear's draughtsmanship coupled with Hullmandel's conscientious workmanship had produced plates of a very high standard, emulated by Gould who was also to employ Hullmandel for many of his folio books.

Lear worked in great detail, outlining every feather and filling in the details with fine lines. This scientific accuracy extended to every part of the bird, from the beak to the claws. He noted on the plate the scale of the bird as shown in relation to its life-size, whenever he had reduced it. Only one bird was figured on each signed and dated plate. More often, only the bird itself was coloured, but occasionally parts of a branch adjacent to the bird figure were also painted. The colouring was done with opaque water-colours with touches of egg-white for parts of the feathers requiring sheen and for the eye to add that "life-touch". The foregrounds were sketches of branches, leaves and twigs only, and no background details were added.

Some of Lear's original pencil drawings, and pen and wash or watercolour sketches are now in the McGill University Library, Montreal. That library owns a number of other drawings besides some of the parrots. These are drawings for the Knowsley Hall birds, and six other aquarelles, dated c1832–5, of eagles, herons and cranes. These latter would most probably be studies for the bird plates used by Gould in his *Birds of Europe* 1832–7.

Gould had adopted the same style and format as Lear's *Parrots* for his own first book, *Century of birds...from the Himalayas* 1831–2. His wife had lithographed their drawings for this work, with Lear's help. Lear says he assisted Mrs Gould with the foregrounds and he drew some of the twigs and leaves in the foregrounds. Like Lear's bird-plates, there were no backgrounds, the birds being perched on twigs or branches. No acknowledgement of Lear's contribution to the plates was made by Gould.

Lear became more heavily committed to helping Gould during a visit they paid to the Continent. They visited a number of zoos and made drawings of birds. Holland, Switzerland and Germany were on their itinerary and during this trip Lear promised to see through the press the parts of Gould's *Birds of Europe*, – a promise which took six years to fulfil. Lear's portion of the work included the larger birds and he was especially facile at reproducing individual portraits of owls and other birds of prey. By this time Gould had adopted much more sophisticated backgrounds to his plates, but Lear's contributions were, nevertheless, characterized by their simple backgrounds. Among Lear's plates are the spotted eagle, the Egyptian and black vultures, a purple heron, demoiselle crane, gannets, rook, wallcreeper, and Tengmalm's owl. On some of these plates may be seen Lear's signature and the date of the original drawing. This did not prevent Gould from attaching the usual "J & E Gould del et lith." label, however.

In 1833 Lear was at work on a quite different group of birds, the toucans. Gould was preparing his first monograph of a bird family and had chosen the Ramphastidae. Lear contributed nine of the plates and also drew the backgrounds of tropical plants for his birds. These flamboyant bird portraits included likenesses of young birds with a pair of adults. The birds were drawn so large they filled the page and were shown in repose with only a head turned to better display the fantastic bills.

Dr Gray of the British Museum had introduced Lear to Lord Stanley when both men were present at a meeting in the Zoological Gardens. Lord Stanley asked Lear to draw some of the animals and birds in his menagerie at Knowsley near Liverpool. Lear lived at Knowsley for many months during the four year period 1832–6 and did over a hundred drawings. Some of these are preserved in the library at Knowsley, others in the library of the University at Montreal. The best drawings were used for a book called *Gleanings from the Menagerie and Aviary at Knowsley Hall*, which was privately printed in 1846. Dr J. E. Gray provided the ten pages of text, mainly from the notes of the Earl of Derby (Lord Stanley succeeded to this title in 1834). Lear's drawings were lithographed by J. W. Moore and the colouring was done by Bayfield. Plates eight to sixteen depicted birds, including four species of guans, an American emu, two cranes and an eyebrowed rollulus. Plate 15 was drawn on the stone by David Mitchell and was a lithotint of a maned goose. The birds are shown against a blue sky, with the background very lightly drawn in, as was Lear's usual practice. The figures themselves are beautifully executed with every feather immaculate. The birds are shown crouching, standing, perching, and are relaxed though not animated.

Whilst Lear had been visiting Knowsley, drawing the animals and birds there, and entertaining the Earl's grandchildren with delightful nonsense verse and stories, he had also done some more drawings for Gould and a few for the wealthy Thomas Campbell Eyton (1809–80). Eyton had written an elaborate *Monograph of the Anatidae or duck tribe*. Among the numerous plates in this treatise are six, hand-coloured, executed from drawings by Lear. These are full-page bird portraits with nearly the whole page being coloured. The sky is pale blue, there is a background of deeper blue and the stones and grass on which the ducks are standing are also coloured. The birds are pedestrian and the plates are examples of pure zoological draughtsmanship rather than artistically designed portraits of members of the duck tribe. The anatomical plates were not done by Lear, and the details of beaks, intestines, etc., though reasonably successful when lithographed, show the limits of the use of this medium, for no lines are crisp or definitive and fine detail is impossible. The numerous wood-engravings in the text show quite clearly how superior is this method of reproducing clear, fine-drawn diagrams.

Just as the drawings for Eyton's book had been executed some time before their publication in 1838, so had Lear's work on Gould's *Monograph of the Trogonidae*, published the same year, been done earlier. This was Gould's second monograph and he was helped in the main by Mrs Gould, Lear contributing no complete plates but assisting with lithographing Mrs Gould's designs.

Lear also gave the Goulds some assistance with the fifty lithographs of birds in Darwin's account of *The Zoology of the voyage of H.M.S. Beagle*, published in 1841, and had two of his drawings lithotinted for G. R. Gray's *Genera of Birds* in volume II 1849. In these cases he had to work from skins and stuffed specimens.

Apart from the above, Lear did a number of drawings which were reproduced by metal-engravings e.g. in the *Zoology* of Captain Beechey's voyage on board the Blossom, Plates iii-xiv; in Sir William Jardine's Naturalist's library, the volumes by Selby on *Pigeons* 1835 and *Parrots* 1836.

The close, exacting work had affected Lear's general health and had also strained his eyes, so that he could no longer continue as a zoological draughts-man. On October 31st 1836 he wrote to Gould, "my eyes are so sadly worse, that no bird under an ostrich shall I soon be able to do."

In 1837 Lear left England for Rome, and for most of the rest of his life lived abroad, earning his living as a landscape painter, writing accounts of his travels and publishing volumes of nonsense verse.

Lear's birds are fascinating insofar as they have decided personalities of their own, sometimes almost whimsical characters. He combined accuracy of portrayal with artistically pleasing design. His birds are not full of life and animation, but neither are they stuffed specimens. His best pictures are those drawn from live models. He stands on the borderline between the stiff portraits of the metal engravers and the freer, softer figures of the lithographers. Much of his work is in the detailed, fine-lined style of the engravers, but his figures are often shown in motion—either moving their heads or walking. His backgrounds are poor—a curious fact considering he was to spend the rest of his life as a landscape painter, but apart from Audubon no other bird-artist of the time was producing full habitat scenes and landscapes for their bird figures. He pointed the way to a freer, livelier depiction of birds by the lithographic method, which was taken a step further by Gould. Indeed, Gould learnt much from Lear, and profited financially, whereas Lear the pioneer, had never been sufficiently rewarded.

Books containing lithographs after drawings by Edward Lear

LEAR, E. Illustrations of the family of Psittacidae, or parrots. 1830–32. 42 plates Autolithographer 42 hand-coloured lithogs.

GOULD, J. A Century of birds from the Himalayan Mountains. 1831 100 plates Assisted Mrs Gould with the hand-col. lithogs.

GOULD, J. A Monograph of the Ramphastidae, or family of toucans. 1834 34 plates (33 col.) Autolithographer 9 hand-col. lithogs.

GOULD, J. Birds of Europe. 1832–7 5 vols. 448 plates Autolithographer a few hand-col. lithogs.

GOULD, J. A Monograph of the Trogonidae or family of trogons. 1838 36 plates Assisted Mrs Gould with the hand-col. lithogs.

DARWIN, C. *editor* The Zoology of the voyage of H.M.S. Beagle 1832–6. 1841 50 plates Assisted Mrs Gould with the hand-col. lithogs.

GRAY, J.E. Gleanings from the menagerie and aviary at Knowsley Hall. 1846. 17 plates Artist Plates 8–16, 7 hand-col. lithogs lithographed by J. W. Moore; 1 lithotint (Plate 15) lithographed by D. W. Mitchell.

GRAY, G.R. Genera of birds. 1844–49 3 vols 335 plates (185 hand-col.) Artist 2 lithotints in vol II.

Caption to Plate facing page 32

Lear's Red-capped Parrakeet (*Platycercus pileatus* from Illustrations of the family of Psittacidae, 1830 Pl. 21) drawn, lithographed and hand-coloured by Lear for the first monograph of a family of birds, when he was 18 years old.

JOHN GOULD

1804-1881

"GOULD'S PLATES", that is how we refer to two thousand nine hundred and ninety-nine hand-coloured lithographs of birds in fourteen great folio books and illustrations in two smaller sized accounts of the zoology of ships' voyages. Most of the plates are in forty-one imperial folio size volumes (approximately 22″ × 16″), the format adopted by Lear and recognised by Gould as being ideal both for lithographic work and depicting birds full-size. Though Gould wrote the texts for most of his books, collected, bought and set-up most of the specimens, arranged the publishing and distribution of the parts, saw them through the press and into the hands of the subscribers he had persuaded to purchase his books, he was no great artist and never learnt lithography. Gould did rough sketches, in pencil, of his birds and festooned them with notes as to the colours of the feathers, position of nostrils, length of bill, etc. He also worked out the designs for his plates right up to the last days of his life. These sketches were transformed into water-colour drawings by his artists and then transferred onto the lithographic stones by them. Nevertheless, Gould deserves the tribute we pay him by referring to "Gould's plates", for he was a remarkable organiser of the changing team which produced those magnificent plates, and his story of success as a businessman and of how he came to be recognised as an ornithologist, is one of the poor boy making good against many odds.

Gould was born on 14th September 1804 in Lyme Regis, Dorset, and educated at Guildford. His father took a job as gardener in the Royal Gardens at Windsor. Gould, when fourteen, was placed in the care of Mr J. T. Aiton, the Head Gardener, to learn the same trade. One of his tasks was to pick dandelions for Queen Charlotte's favourite tea. In his spare time he caught and stuffed birds and so learnt the art of taxidermy at which he became very proficient. In his own collection of stuffed birds there were a couple of magpies, shot and beautifully set-up when he was still only fourteen years old. He also became an expert egg-blower and kept the boys at Eton supplied with birds' eggs and bird specimens. He left Windsor, and for a short time was with Sir William Ingleby at Ripley Castle, Yorkshire. In his 20th year he moved to London. By a stroke of good fortune, the newly-formed Zoological Society of London required a taxidermist. In 1827 Gould obtained the post of curator of birds and chief taxidermist on the strength of his ability to produce well set-up birds. When George IV's giraffe died, a few months after it was brought to England, Gould turned his attention from birds for some time and took on the job of stuffing the giraffe. This was perhaps his most notable example of the art of taxidermy, but he stuffed a very large number of birds and maintained this interest throughout his subsequent career.

In 1829 Gould married Miss Elizabeth Coxen, the daughter of Captain Nicholas Coxen of Kent. She was the same age as Gould and had been educated as a governess. She was, moreover, very artistic. Her drawings had a degree of charm which made them immediately attractive. This quality was to be of vital importance to the way their future developed.

The year after his marriage, Gould was fortunate enough to obtain possession of a very fine collection of birds from the hill countries of India, the exact source was not disclosed. This was the first collection of any size to reach Europe from the Himalayas and Gould decided to make the most of the opportunity it offered and to issue an illustrated book describing the rarest of the species among the skins which he had stuffed and set up on perches. It was difficult. He was not, at this stage, sufficiently versed in the language of ornithologists, or skilled in the science of species identification and description, to write the text. Only with great effort and concentration could he draw the outline sketches of birds, though he was acquiring the ability to make quick rough sketches. So, Gould did what he was to do for the rest of his life, he organised other people to use their skills and then used their work to produce one of his own. His friend and mentor, Nicholas Aylward Vigors, who was an ardent supporter of the Zoological Society and its Secretary from 1826 to 1832, described the birds and named the new species. The scientific descriptions were published in the first edition of the *Proceedings* of the Zoological Society in 1831. Among these new birds was a beautiful sunbird, which Vigors named *Aethyopyga gouldiae* after Mrs Gould. Her husband showed his wife his sketches and said she could learn how to transfer them onto lithographic stones. This was most probably not the first time, and certainly it would not be the last, that Gould was to calmly tell his wife that she was about to do what she thought impossible. However, she learned to draw directly onto the stones from his sketches and did so very satisfactorily. She worked in the rooms of the Zoological Society in Bruton Street where she and her husband lived.

Having got as far as that, Gould went in search of a publisher, but failed to find one willing to take the risk of publishing an unknown bird-man's folio-sized plates, even if the respected N. A. Vigors had written the text. Gould reluctantly decided to be his own publisher. It so happened, that this proved the most effective way of keeping full control over his book production and he continued to publish his own work to the end of his life. Gould solicited his subscribers and then, at his own expense, commenced issuing the parts of *A Century of Birds* in 1831. Mrs Gould drew one hundred and two figures of birds (the two exceeding the hundred being young males of species already figured) on eighty lithographic plates which, when printed, were coloured by hand. A leaf of text accompanying each plate or in a few cases, two or three of the plates, gave the description of the birds in Latin, the measurements, history, habitat and habits of the birds in English. The plates included a detail of the claw, etc., where such features were unusual or distinctive. There were no backgrounds, the only detail besides the birds being a tree stump, branch, etc., in the foreground. The book is found in three states, one with both bird and foreground coloured, another with only the birds coloured, and a third in monochrome. The twenty monthly parts were completed in August 1832. The venture turned out to be a success and Gould made some money on it. It deserved its success, since it was the most accurately illustrated work on foreign ornithology published up to that date.

Gould had adopted many of Lear's ideas—folio-sized plates to show the birds life-size, publishing the work himself, and getting that excellent printer of lithographic plates, Charles Hullmandel, to print from Mrs Gould's stones. Unlike poor, struggling Lear, he had made a profit, despite having had to employ so many other people to do the work. Lear had found one hundred and seventy-five subscribers for his *Parrots*, whereas Gould had two hundred and ninety-eight when *Century of Birds* reached completion (in later years the number totalled three hundred and thirty-five).

Gould had not yet established himself as a serious ornithologist, and he never achieved real competence at identification of birds in the field. Indeed, Professor Newton went so far as to say that "he has no personal knowledge of any English birds, except those found between Eton and Maidenhead, and about those species he fancies no one else knows anything." There must have been some truth in this accusation since when Gould and Wolf went on field trips together, it was usually Wolf who identified the species which they saw and found their nests. There was a further serious limitation to Gould's ability as an ornithologist. It is apparent that he never troubled himself unduly with the study of systematic ornithology. But he did over the years acquire a great deal of knowledge of different bird forms and he could discriminate minute specific differences between allied forms. This ability only developed gradually, but the number of skins which passed through his hands greatly facilitated the learning process. By the time he was forty he was regarded by fellow scientists as an "ornithologist" and not just as a taxidermist and bird-man.

He had an insatiable appetite for new specimens and could be somewhat unscrupulous in his efforts to get hold of any unique or rare form. Nearly all of the new skins of humming-birds which reached London found their way into his hands. Wolf said that if he wanted a bird which a friend had, that friend needed to be very ingenious to frustrate Gould's attempts to "borrow" the skin, since once in Gould's possession it would never be seen again. Wolf had the skin of a young, very dark, male Norwegian falcon which got into Gould's box and somehow never found its way out again. If Gould saw a bird he wanted at a dealer's, he would not betray his mounting excitement, but would casually remark, "I think I have that; but I wish you would lend it to me to compare." The unsuspecting dealer would lend Gould the skin. Gould would then dash home and get Mrs Gould, or later Wolf, to make a sketch of the bird, and then return the skin to the dealer. He was most economical, and though he loved possessing the specimens, he did not part with his money needlessly. This love of collecting birds stayed with him throughout his life and Dr R. B. Sharpe said, "It was always a real pleasure to see the delight which animated the old naturalist when, in his invalid days, I took him some startling new form of bird...".

In the 1830s Gould visited the principal European museums, so keen was he to search for, and extend his knowledge of, new bird forms, particularly those which were then unknown in Britain. On at least one trip, Edward Lear accompanied Gould and helped him to make drawings of birds in the museums and zoos of Holland, Germany and Switzerland. No doubt Gould also benefitted still further from these foreign visits by becoming acquainted with European ornithologists. One of these friends was the Director of Leyden Museum, Professor C. J. Temminck, who was then engaged in the publication of a fine set of coloured plates of birds (*Nouveau receuil de planches coloriées d'oiseaux*, 1820–38 with 600 coloured copper-engravings).

Gould freely used the specimens in his own and other collections both in

England and Europe for his next book which was called *The Birds of Europe*. He started issuing the twenty-two parts in 1832 and finished five years later. It is believed that Edward Lear had helped Mrs Gould with some of the foregrounds in *Century of Birds*. We have clearer evidence of his assistance in *Birds of Europe* since a number of the plates bear his signature and the year in which he executed the original water-colour. In a letter written to his friend, Chichester Fortescue, Lear stated, "I assisted Mrs Gould in all her drawings of foregrounds, as may be seen in a moment by anyone who will glance at my drawings in Gould's European birds and toucans." The large majority of the four hundred and forty-eight hand-coloured lithographs in *Birds of Europe* were done by Mrs Gould, and all were printed by Hullmandel. In this book a few nests are included in the plates, both the marsh and penduline tits being shown with their nests, though no juvenile birds appear. These plates have some foreground details and the bird perched on an isolated branch, or on a rock. The background is merely a blue wash or tint. The foregrounds are coloured. Gradually the Gouldian plate formula is evolving. We shall see that as the titles succeed one another there are small innovations introduced at successive stages until the full tableau, or composition of the bird plates, emerges, and is used by Gould for his later books and then adopted by Gould's successors.

Whilst busy with *Birds of Europe*, Gould started work on his first monograph. He chose the toucan family, a group of colourful, though ungraceful, birds whose main characteristic is an enormous bill. Their bills are usually coloured with several bright hues. Their curious name comes from the Tupi Indians of Brazil who call them "tucano" and they are birds of the tropical forests of America. Lear did nine of these birds and Mr and Mrs Gould the other twenty-four coloured plates. Most of the specimens were shown with their heads turned sideways in order to display the bill. On a few of the plates depicting the pair of the species, a young bird was added. There were also some lovely tropical plants in these pictures. Gould later issued a supplement adding twenty-one plates and a second edition in the 1850s when Richter lithographed the new species discovered since Gould completed the first edition.

Gould took only two years to issue the three parts of *Monograph of the Ramphastidae*, or toucans, so he was able to start work on his trogons in 1836. He issued the thirty-six plates in three parts to one hundred and seventy-five subscribers in the months of 1836–8. This book dealt with thirty-four species and was a remarkable achievement since only twelve of these species had been previously known to science. Gould the scientist is beginning to emerge. The plates by the author and his wife included a double plate spread of a life-size quetzel. This book, like that about the toucans, was very popular and Gould issued a second edition in the 1850s. Gould loved these highly coloured birds. The males are extremely gaudy, very similar in all of the species, with the breast and abdomen bright red, pink, yellow, or orange, and have long graduated tails. The tail of the resplendent trogon was too long for the folio sized plate and Gould had to have an elongated sheet of paper, folded up at the bottom, to accommodate the bird's tail. The birds are depicted in pairs, which shows the different plumage clearly. The later edition, 1858–75, with lithographs by Richter and Hart have some birds flying and some with insects, with smaller figures of the birds themselves in the background, in contrast with the simpler designs for the plates of the first edition. This second edition is altogether more elaborate with the addition of florid tropical plants and many young birds of the species discovered in the twenty years since the earlier publication. Issued in three parts, this new edition contained new drawings of the birds figured in the first edition plus eighteen additional figures of new species. A supplement a year later added a further twenty plates and by that time the trogons were well represented and described.

In 1837 Gould started on a new book whilst *Birds of Europe* was in the final stages. This was typical of Gould's manner of working. His restless energy could only find an outlet by having many irons in the fire at one and the same time. His newest idea was to issue a description of new species as they were discovered and brought to Europe from all over the world. He called this miscellany of birds *Icones avium*. Most probably, this would have developed into a bird journal with periodic issues describing and figuring new birds, but after two parts had been issued, Gould embarked on his great Australian adventure and *Icones avium* was abandoned. It is interesting, because it shows further progress in his plate design. In the eighteen plates, which form a kind of supplement to his previous books, some birds have quite elaborate backgrounds, though others have hardly any. More insects are being shown and in addition, some claw details are given. The Gouldian pattern for the text, now being written by Gould himself, is well-established. For each species Gould wrote a leaf of textual matter, containing a diagnosis of the bird, in Latin (copied from the original description, usually compiled by another scientist), a description in English, a synonymy and brief information of the history and geography of the species. In *Icones avium* Part I there were ten of Mrs Gould's plates. In Part II, issued a year later in 1838, the eight plates virtually form a monograph of the *Caprimulgidae* since they are figures of the nightjars.

JOHN GOULD

Charles Darwin's famous *Zoology of the voyage of H.M.S. Beagle* was published in the 1830s. The third volume dealt with the birds seen and collected on the voyage. In it, Darwin gave notice of the species' habits and ranges, and G. R. Gray of the British Museum did most of the work of identification of the species. The text was partly written by Gould, but he did not complete his share of the work. The fifty quarto-size hand-coloured plates were executed by Mrs Gould from sketches by her husband. This volume is thought to be the only one in which all the lithographs are entirely the work of Mr and Mrs Gould.

Gould's attention had been caught by some very colourful birds from Australia which Mrs Gould's two emigrant brothers, Charles and Stephen Coxen, had sent from New South Wales. Mrs Gould had made water-colour studies of these specimens, many of which were new birds. Gould started publishing a *Synopsis of the Birds of Australia* in 1837. Four parts were issued with seventy-three lithographs showing the heads of the one hundred and sixty-eight different species. In a few cases, the outlines of the whole bird, a wing, or the feet were drawn in with pencil. At this time the birds of the great Continent of Australia were still almost unknown. Previously, there had been some notices in periodicals of new species, John Lewin had written his *Birds of New Holland* and illustrated it with some copper-engravings in 1808, and one part of a book, later abandoned by its authors Vigors and Horsfield, had described the species of Australian birds in the collection of the Linnean Society. Gould's own *The Birds of Australia and adjacent islands* only ran to two parts before he abandoned it. He and Mrs Gould had done twenty plates when Gould realised that he needed more specimens to carry on with the job of recording and figuring Australian birds.

His brothers-in-law were farming and trying to establish themselves in the new country so could not spare the time to trek in the bush and find more birds. The enterprising Gould decided he must go and get his specimens himself. The financial returns on his books had been so good that he had made £7,000 over the past eight years, so he could afford to make the trip. Mrs Gould would have to go as well in order to make her drawings on the spot. They now had four children, but the three youngest would have to stay behind and be looked after by Mrs Gould's mother. Gould had consulted a rudimentary map of Australia and was aware that he needed an assistant to cover so vast an area, so he appointed John Gilbert, a zoologist, at a salary of £100 per annum plus all expenses, to go with them.

The party embarked on the four month sea voyage to Australia in May 1838. Gould was not idle on the voyage, but used the ship's boat, when the weather was calm, to collect some thirty species of ocean birds. He made many observations of their range and added a good deal to our knowledge of the petrels. He even did some experimental bird-ringing. He caught a number of black-browed albatrosses with a hook and line and put rings on their legs. Many of the birds he caught the following day, one hundred and thirty miles nearer Australia, bore his rings.

When he landed in Van Diemen's Land, or Tasmania, Gould set about collecting the fauna and flora and became an explorer too when he pushed his way further into the bush than other white men had penetrated hitherto. Mrs Gould remained in Hobart Town, in a cottage in the grounds of the governor's residence. The governor at that time was Sir John Franklin the Arctic explorer. Mrs Gould was kept very busy drawing plants and birds. Whilst in Hobart her fifth child was born, and named Franklin after their kind hosts. Gould had been returning at intervals with his collections, packing some of them up and sending them to England and leaving some with his wife for sketches to be made. In August 1839 they all moved to New South Wales and stayed with Mrs Gould's brothers at Yarrundi in the valley of the Hunter River. From here Gould explored the surrounding countryside and collected more birds in South Australia.

Gould sent Gilbert to the west of Australia in January 1839. Gilbert worked hard and was successful in finding hundreds of different species, many of them new. Between 1838 and 1845 (Gilbert stayed on in Australia until 1841, and then after a short stay in England, returned again in 1842) Gilbert visited every one of the Australian states and sent thousands of specimens to Gould.

In April the Goulds sailed for England and arrived in September. Gould had already made up a list of subscribers for *Birds of Australia* before leaving England and had added forty-six names whilst in Australia. He lost no time in issuing his first part, with eighteen plates and descriptive letterpress, in December 1840—just three months after his arrival back home. He charged £3/3/0 per part and issued four parts each year. His publishing machinery worked like clockwork, and it needed to at this particular time since his trip to Australia had cost him about £2,000 and he needed to recoup this.

Among the packages which were awaiting him, sent from Australia, were skins, eggs, nests and specimens of young birds. Gould and Gilbert were very thorough in their work. Through their efforts about three hundred new species were added to those birds already known to inhabit Australasia. In the thirty-six parts of *Birds of Australia* were six hundred plates done from the drawings of John and Elizabeth Gould. The birds were not all from Australia, but included some sent from New Zealand and New Guinea. The specimens continued to arrive as the publication was in progress. They came from many naturalist friends Gould had made in Australia, and from officers of various ships visiting the area and from other collectors willing to lend their specimens such as F. Strange of Sydney, who sent the bird Owen's kiwi.

The plates accurately portrayed the 36 *Accipitres*, 311 *Passeres*, 36 *Scansores*, 23 *Columbae*, 16 *Grallinae*, 1 *Struthiones*, 78 *Grallae* and 99 *Anseres*, as the birds were classified in those days. A few juveniles, nests and eggs were included, and the pair of the species. When both sexes were similarly plumaged, a front and back view of the birds was depicted. The food was often shown, berries, insects, etc., being included. There were some habitat backgrounds, but more often the native plants were carefully delineated in the foreground and there was little other embellishment of the picture. Some of the subjects were shown in unnatural surroundings. The text is much more detailed than in Gould's previous books, because he added notes from his own observations of the birds in the field. He also drew heavily on Gilbert's notes on bird behaviour, distribution, habitat, etc., and acknowledged his source. He gives many interesting indications as to where he obtained his specimens in the instances when he had shot them himself. Since he had no time to write a journal, any idea as to the extent of his travels must be gleaned from these comments.

When naming the many new species, Gould frequently used the names of royalty (Prince Albert's Lyrebird *Menura alberti* 1850 and the Victoria Riflebird *Ptiloris victoriae* 1849 out of gratitude for Her Majesty's agreeing to his dedicating *Birds of Australia* to his Queen), names of officials in Australia who had helped him, and his friends e.g. one bird was named after his wife's brother, Charles Coxen (1809–76) who was also an ornithologist in his own right. This was the small fig-parrot or blue-browed lorikeet *Opopsitta coxeni* of 1867. Gould usually first described his new species at meetings of the Zoological Society, the account being published in the *Proceedings*. Later in life he gave the first account of new birds in other magazines, e.g. *Annals and Magazine of Natural History*. The descriptions were then repeated in his books.

Among the islands of Van Diemen's Gulf, Gilbert found a new finch with vivid colouring in yellow, purple, green and red. He sent it to Gould from Greenhill Island and Gould named it *Poephila gouldiae* after his wife. It became known as the Gouldian painted finch and is a testimony to Gould's gratitude to his wife who had so devotedly supported him in Australia and helped him with his work. It is also a sad reminder of a tragic event in Gould's life. Eleven months after their return from Australia, Elizabeth Gould died. She was only thirty-seven years old. In their twelve years of married life she had done six hundred drawings for him, borne him six children and accompanied him on his journey to Australia sharing all the discomforts and danger that such an epic voyage entailed at that time. Gould was ambitious, persevering and very industrious, but without his wife's devotion and help and her artistic ability, also her own enthusiasm and hard work, in the very early stages of his career, he would not have achieved his early success. Gould never failed to tell his friends and associates how much he owed to his wife's courage, devotion and artistic aptitude, and he wrote a warm appreciation of her in the introduction to *Birds of Australia* (the introduction was published after the last part had been issued, the usual practice when books were issued in parts.)

The year 1841 was very bleak for Gould. He must have felt that his whole life, including his career, had been shattered by the death of his wife. Without a sympathetic artist and lithographer he could not go on with his own work, and his livelihood was at stake. He was in the middle of an immense project, with subscribers expecting further parts of *Birds of Australia* to be delivered to them each quarter. Gould had to search hard and long for a satisfactory lithographer to transfer his own and his wife's remaining sketches onto the stones. He could not ask Lear, since he had left England in 1837, and Swainson also had gone abroad. Apart from Mrs Gould, they were the only two who had proved themselves capable of lithographing birds.

When sketching the birds for sixteen quarto plates in the account of the *Zoology of the voyage of H.M.S. Sulphur*, issued 1843–44, Gould had the services of Benjamin Waterhouse Hawkins, but he did not employ this fine lithographer for his folios. The man he eventually found was H. C. Richter, who turned out to be more than adequate for the job. How Gould found Richter, or what Richter had been doing before he met Gould, we do not know. We know little else about Henry Constantine Richter except that he died at Frithville Gardens, Hammersmith, on the 16th March 1902 aged 81, from influenza after a short illness.

Richter completed the lithographic work on the six hundred plates in *Birds of Australia* in 1848. Gould still had more specimens, sufficient for Richter to execute a further eighty-one plates for a supplement. This included birds from every Australian state, New Zealand and Lord Howe Island. Much of the material had been sent by John Gilbert, but in 1845 Gilbert tragically lost his life in the bush when a native's spear struck him. Gould was very upset at the loss of Gilbert. He was further distressed by the loss of another of his

J. and E. Gould

NARINE TROGON
Trogon Narina; (Shaw)

collectors, Johnson Drummond, who was murdered by natives in Western Australia. A third collector was fatally wounded when a gun exploded whilst he was landing from a boat on a Bass Strait island.

Despite these vicissitudes, Gould worked on and made his *Birds of Australia* a success. He also planned a monograph of American partridges, which he commenced in 1844. He and Richter did thirty-two plates for the three parts, issued at quite long intervals, in 1844, 1846 and 1850. Gould wrote about the various species in greater detail than usual. The male and female of each species was delineated, and a lot of cryptically marked chicks were also included in the most attractive plates.

By this time the Gould "plate formula" was being applied consistently in his folios. This consisted of a plate showing the pair of a species, or, if the birds were too large for them both to be shown on one plate, the first plate was used for the male and a second showed the female bird. Where the sexes were similarly plumaged, both a dorsal and ventral view was painted. The plate might include a nest, a nest with eggs in it, or a chick, if these were available at the time the drawing was made and if they could be fitted into the composition of the pictures. This was important, since Gould's designs for his plates were essentially pictures of the birds, with the stress on composition as opposed to the diagrammatic approach of earlier bird-book illustrators. Sometimes, indeed, the bird figures are subservient to the completed tableau. Gould gave little or no background detail, usually being satisfied with a blue tinted background as for sky. The foreground was sometimes quite elaborate when Gould was interested in the terrain or the plants, e.g. plant food would be drawn carefully, whereas grasses would be shown as a green mass. Often the foreground was quite simple, with a few rocks for a sea-shore, or a wall as a complement to the figures of swallows, wall-creepers, etc. The habitat, when shown, is often, though not always, a clue as to the lithographer. Mrs Gould had started with no background, then moved towards the inclusion of plants and branches. Lear drew in the merest suggestion of the landscape and terrain, Richter delighted in doing leaves and flowers and is much more painstaking over the foreground scenes.

Richter had a great deal to do with one of Gould's most successful publications, the *Monograph of the Trochilidae* 1849–61, which was issued in twenty-five parts. The three hundred and sixty plates of humming-birds were drawn on the stone by Richter from sketches by Gould. Usually each plate had one pair of birds, with an occasional nest or young bird, though there were a few plates with pairs of different species. Nearly all the plates have at least one bird in flight, thus showing every part of the beautiful plumage of these tiny birds. Gould had received specimens from all parts of The New World since he first started collecting humming-birds—enough subjects to fill six volumes with four hundred and eighteen plates (including the supplement). His daughter said that their Victorian drawing-room, with cream walls and gold and pale-blue curtains which her mother had planned, gradually became filled to overflowing with cases of humming-birds as her father's collection grew and he took it over as his study. Gould saw his first live humming-bird in Philadelphia when on a short visit to America in 1857.

At the time of the Great Exhibition, 1851, Gould mounted a set of these birds in glass cases and exhibited them in a building he was given permission to erect in the gardens of the Zoological Society. In this display he also demonstrated how he used pure gold leaf over-painted with transparent oil colours and varnish to copy the irridescent colours of the humming-birds' feathers. Gould, shrewd businessman that he was, must have realised what good publicity for his books this exhibition would prove. He found many subscribers for the *Monograph of Trochilidae*. His financial return for admitting the public to this exhibition, at sixpence a time, was a clear £800.

The same summer, W. Hart first did some work for Gould. William Hart, whose life is unrecorded, was first known as a colourer of ornithological book plates. Hart liked intensely coloured plates, and this characteristic, perhaps more than any other, recommended him to the notice of Gould who was fond of highly coloured birds. Hart made the patterns for the humming-birds and coloured the metallic parts of the plates.

Gould had always got so many projects on hand, that any help he could get from artists and lithographers was welcome. When Wolf arrived in England in 1848, Gould would dearly have liked to include him in his team, but Wolf was as strong a personality as Gould and was going to have no one as his master. Wolf proved so successful himself, that he did not require a patron. Gould admired Wolf and recognised his fine qualities as a bird-artist, but Wolf described Gould as "the most uncouth man I ever knew". Wolf added another comment on Gould's character which is very revealing. He said that Gould would take a new specimen round to Wolf's studio to be delineated, and whilst Wolf was busy, Gould paced up and down the studio, puffing away at a cigar. Evidently Gould never sat down or kept still—except when fishing.

The drawings Gould had from Wolf were lithographed mainly by Richter. In *Birds of Asia* and *Birds of Great Britain* seventy-nine plates bore Wolf's signature, only a handful of them lithographed by Hart. *Birds of Asia* had been started in 1850 and Richter laboured for years on the plates for the parts.

JOHN GOULD

He transferred Gould's sketches onto the stones and was able to supplement these drawings with studies from live specimens e.g. when Gould received a present of two live Temminck's tragopans. For other plates, specimens were all that he had to work from, and Gould's sketches showing the design for the plate. Richter's interest in plants is in evidence in many of the plates, including that illustrating a black-headed bunting where the figure is perched on a wild hop plant. Most of the birds illustrated came from India where such noted naturalists as Blyth and Jerdon had formed extensive collections.

Gould had, up to now, issued avifaunas of foreign continents and monographs of exotic, highly-coloured birds. In 1860 he decided it was time a really good book on British birds was published. He declared that the birds of Great Britain had never been properly illustrated. This was not true. He was overlooking Selby's magnificent *Illustrations of British Ornithology* with life-size coloured engravings of birds, published 1823–33 on plates even larger than those Gould used. However, Gould's *Birds of Great Britain*, issued in twenty-five parts 1862–73 did add a great deal to our knowledge of British birds, besides being a more complete set of pictures of our native birds than previously printed. Furthermore, for the first time we have a lot of chicks, eggs and nests depicted. This title is outstanding for the attention paid to the young of the species. Gould had searched high and low for specimens of the nestlings of rare species and their nests. Wherever possible, drawings were done from freshly killed specimens. The result is that this book has much more lively birds than in Gould's previous folios, and there is much more freedom in showing the birds in different attitudes. Gould did the sketches himself, Hart and Richter did the full-scale water-colours and then the two lithographers drew the patterns on the stone. They did this by developing Gould's sketches and then preparing the drawings with lithographic pencil on oil paper for transfer onto the stones, unlike Mrs Gould who appears to have drawn direct onto the stones from her husband's or her own sketches. Wolf's fifty-seven drawings were lithographed, with foregrounds added, by both lithographers. The foregrounds are close-up scenes of the species' natural haunts.

Five hundred copies of Gould's *Birds of Great Britain*, described as his high-water mark in publishing by one critic, were printed. The illustrations show Gould's work at its best and it demonstrated the work of all his artists and lithographers except Lear and Mrs Gould. Lord Lilford, when preparing a similar work, fifteen years later, wrote of Gould's book, "For really beautiful and correct illustrations of British birds, you will find Gould's great work on that special subject in the library, but the books are so large that you will require a boy to help you carry them from the house." Few owners of *Birds of Great Britain* today would be willing to allow anyone to carry the seven volumes, now worth some £8,000, "from the house", with or without the help of a boy.

With the completion of *Birds of Great Britain*, H. C. Richter's work for Gould came to an end. He had been with Gould during the most productive, middle period of Gould's work, and yet we know nothing about him. His plates show very fine lithographic work, a sensitive approach and a better understanding of the importance of habitat scenes than earlier lithographers. Together, Richter and Gould developed the lithographic bird print a further stage by the inclusion of appropriate terrain and with the addition of many nests and chicks.

In 1870 Gould issued a list of subscribers to, and possessors of, his books. Over one thousand people, institutions and libraries subscribed to one or more of his titles. He calculated that at one point in time his subscription list amounted to £143,000. Understandably, he had more subscribers for *Birds of Great Britain* (397) than for any other title. As the full set cost £78/15/– this was a considerable achievement. His first book, *Century of Birds* was next with 328 subscribers, then the *Humming-birds* with 296 and *Birds of Europe* which had 282 subscribers each paying £76/8/–. The *Birds of Australia* was very expensive at £115 but had attracted 238 subscribers willing to buy it. The *Trogons* and *American partridges* just about paid their way with 167 and 135 subscribers respectively. On the first of January 1866 Gould, in a prospectus, could boast 1008 people on his subscription list, but the "quality" of those personages is the most amazing thing about the list. There were no fewer than twelve monarchs; eleven imperial, serene or royal highnesses; 16 English dukes and duchesses; 6 marquises and marchionesses; 30 earls; 5 counts, countesses and barons; 10 viscounts; the Bishop of Worcester (the only bishop); 36 lords; 31 honourables and 61 baronets. They were subscribing to nine ornithological works, those mentioned above plus *Birds of Asia* and the *Monograph of Ramphastidae* and one of the two books on animals which Gould issued, *Mammals of Australia*, published in 1860 in three volumes. Most of these books were being issued in parts costing £3/3/– each, a price beyond ordinary people in the 19th century.

William Hart was now Gould's chief lithographer, and artist too. He made the water-colour drawings and drew them on the stones, working to Gould's designs. He also coloured the finished prints. From the 22nd part of *Birds of Great Britain*, Hart drew on the stones the designs for the last parts and then went on to assist Gould with some supplements and second editions of earlier titles. Hart did not confine his interests to Gould's work, however, but is known to have continued with his chief occupation as a colourer of plates. He coloured bird plates for both Dresser and Shelley.

From the commencement of work on Gould's new book *Birds of New Guinea*, Hart was involved. The project began publication in 1875 and Hart had lithographed 141 of Gould's sketches up to 1881 when Dr R. B. Sharpe took over the work of finishing the last parts, bringing the total number of plates to three hundred and thirty in 1888. A considerable amount of information had already been published by foreign ornithologists on the avifauna of New Guinea, e.g. Count Salvadori of Italy had enumerated 1030 species from this region and only 320 species were figured in Gould's book, several of these being Australian species. Since the last part of his *Supplement to Birds of Australia* appeared in 1869 Gould used *Birds of New Guinea* to report new discoveries from Australia. These new birds included three bower-birds, the tooth-billed, Queensland and large-frilled. Gould himself considered that his original description of the habits of bower-birds was the most interesting and valuable of his ornithological discoveries. For other birds, Gould and Hart worked from live models in the Zoological Society Gardens whenever possible. The blue-thighed lory *Domicella tibialis* had its portrait done whilst residing at the zoo. Dr Meyer found Meyer's bronze cuckoo *Chalcites meyerii* in the New Guinea Highlands and Hart used his specimen, drawing in an imaginary New Guinea scene, for the plate of this bird. The young cuckoo is shown in a nest of the black and white wren warbler *Malurus alboscapulatus*. A. R. Wallace was at this time collecting birds in the Malayan Peninsula and among other plates in this book showing birds he had found was one of an elegant pitta brought back from an expedition to Lombok. Gould had first described this bird in 1857. Wallace also collected the red-naped pitta. Another bird-collector working in the mountains of New Guinea was Andrew Goldie who collected the red-capped streaked lory, which Sharpe named after him *Psitteuteles goldiei*.

From the middle of the 1870s Gould's health was failing, and he suffered from a painful disease. He never ceased to work and to plan further books. He was keen on writing an oology of the birds of Australia and he commenced a new book about the Pittidae whilst four or five other titles were still in progress. The first part of the *Pittidae* had ten plates, most of which had appeared in the *Birds of New Guinea* and *Birds of Asia* whilst the remaining plates were very similar to others already published by Gould. This use of earlier plates for a new work was not uncommon. Gould actually issued 3325 coloured plates in his folio editions but 326 of them were duplicated. This was the only part of *Monograph of the Pittidae* which Gould saw printed and the book was never completed. When he was confined to his sofa, he still worked on and took a great interest in any new specimens brought to him. The end came, at his home in Charlotte Street near the British Museum, on 3rd February 1881.

Gould's life had been hard, but successful. Though not a particularly happy life, since he never got over the death of his wife and was further saddened by the deaths of two of his sons, he had persevered and in his last years had become admired and greatly respected. Many honours had been showered on him. He had been elected Fellow of the Royal Society in 1843. He became a Fellow of the Zoological Society and for many years was a member of the council and vice-president. He had come a long way since those early days when he was taxidermist to the society. Despite these honours and achievements, Gould seems not to have been liked. The various comments of his associates on his character are not flattering. Only Dr R. B. Sharpe wrote in a really kindly spirit about him. A complicated personality emerges from all these accounts. He had a business-like approach to life, with downright, even brusque, manners. Under this stern, abrasive exterior, he had a kind heart. Dr Sharpe's account of Gould's visits to his secretary when both of them were ill show a kindlier side to his nature. Edwin C. Prince had been a faithful secretary for very many years before his death in 1858, and Gould valued him highly. Though ill himself, Gould had driven every day to see Prince and had, moreover, taken with him anything he thought might do Prince good. This is in sharp contrast to the picture of the Gould who never bought a specimen if he could borrow it, and who turned an honest penny at every available opportunity.

Relations with his business associates were straightforward, with Gould paying promptly for any service rendered. Once having paid for a lithographic drawing, or an artist's drawing, Gould regarded it as his own and attached his own signature when it was printed. Gould has been castigated for this practice, but since he did the rough sketches and designed the plates, he had some right to claim it, at least partly, as his work. His plates bear footnotes such as "J & E Gould del et lith", "J. Gould & H. C. Richter del et lith", and "J. Gould & W. Hart del et lith", all of which are fair. Also quite truthful are the labels "J. Wolf & H. C. Richter del et lith", Gould giving credit where it was due. Underneath plates bearing the signature "E. Lear del 1833" the credits "J & E Gould del et lith" are clearly wrong and the artist concerned felt justifiably annoyed. Lear's assessment of Gould must be read in the light of this knowledge of Lear's complaint. Lear said of Gould, "He was one I never liked really, for in spite of a certain jollity and bonhommie, he was a harsh and violent man. At the Zoological Society at 33 Bruton Street, at Hullmandel's—at Broad Street ever the same, persevering hard working toiler in his own line,—but ever as unfeeling for those about him. In this earliest phase of his bird-drawing he owes everything to his excellent wife, & myself,—without whose help in drawing he had done nothing." Gould was left without his wife and Lear's help in 1841 and went on, building on their firm foundation, to achieve even greater success. Even if his associates did not greatly care for him, nor he for them, it is undeniable that each member of that team worked for him for many years.

Gould had left a number of books unfinished. The entire stock of Gould's works and copyrights was purchased by the firm of Henry Sotheran & Co., who took over the publication of the unfinished books, Dr R. B. Sharpe undertook the writing of the text and Hart completed the additional plates necessary to make the monographs as complete as possible. The *Birds of Asia* had to be brought to a close after the thiry-fifth part was finished, the last three parts being done by Sharpe and Hart, whilst the first thirty-two parts had been the work of Gould and Richter. Hart had also to become artist as well as lithographer. Gould had been working on a supplement to his monumental work on humming-birds when he died. These were the first birds with which Hart had helped Gould, so it was natural that Dr Sharpe should leave the plates of the supplement to Hart. After the first part, which Gould had seen through the press, Hart did the drawings, lithography and colouring for the remainder of the fifty-eight plates, issued 1880–7. Nearly all of these birds are shown in flight, and in pairs. Dr Sharpe wrote the text for the species not dealt with by Gould, and Osbert Salvin had oversight of the whole work.

Hart continued to work for Dr Sharpe after they had brought Gould's work to a close. He paid great attention to background material in the illustrations for his later books and his painting of leaves was particularly detailed. The last time we have evidence of Hart's work is in the London edition of Elliot's *Monograph of the Pittidae* published 1893–5, where some plates are signed "W. Hart del et lith". These showed the main feature of Hart's work— a bold execution. He was less accurate than Richter and not as fine a lithographer. He tended to over-colour his work—a factor quite acceptable to Gould but liable to be criticised severely today. He is seen at his best with the colourful tropical birds, perhaps his most outstanding plates being those depicting birds of paradise.

Of original drawings and sketches done for the 2999 plates, the whereabouts of only a handful are known. Available to the public in this country is one Gould item in the Print Room at the British Museum. The sheet ($9\frac{3}{4}'' \times 14\frac{7}{8}''$) has two quails with their young on the ground among grasses and blue convolvulus, inscribed "Quail. J. Gould 1863" and signed and dated a second time, "J. Gould F. R. S. March 11, 1864", in pencil and water-colour. On the reverse, is a pencil sketch of two robins. In the Zoological Library of the British Museum (Natural History) there are some drawings relating to Australian birds, attributed to Gould. More items are now in the McGill University Library, Montreal. This library has twenty-two bird portraits done in watercolours. They have marginal notes in Mrs Gould's handwriting and are dated 1831–6. A few others are in the hands of private owners. Nine portfolios of the original notes written by Gould in Australia, with his rough sketches of birds, or parts of birds, are in the Balfour Library, the Department of Zoology, University of Cambridge.

Gould's bird specimens, of which there were thousands, were variously distributed. Before his death he had offered the British Museum his Australian bird skins for the sum of £1,000, but the Trustees had refused them. Gould sold them instead to an American, Thomas B. Wilson, for the Academy of Natural Science in Philadelphia. The British Museum bought his wonderful collection of 5,000 humming-birds after his death for £3,000 together with the rest of his collections. Anyone visiting the British Museum to look at Gould's birds can see for themselves what a fine taxidermist Gould had been.

His taxidermy had been a side-line. It is incredible to think that besides that and all the work outlined here, Gould had also been the author, or editor, of over three hundred notes, articles and papers for scientific periodicals and had also issued a *Monograph of the Kangaroos*.

John Gould was fond of quoting some words, used jokingly by a close friend when introducing Gould to a relative, which form a fitting epitaph for him, "Here lies John Gould, the Bird Man".

Books containing "Gould's plates" in order of publication
(folio size unless stated otherwise: all hand-coloured lithographs)

GOULD, J. A century of birds hitherto unfigured, from the Himalaya Mountains. Text by N. A. Vigors 1831–2 80 plates Rough sketches by Gould, autolithographs by E. Gould.

GOULD, J. The birds of Europe 1832–7 5 vols. 448 plates Artists: J. & E. Gould, E. Lear Lithographers: E. Gould & E. Lear.

JOHN GOULD

GOULD, J. A monograph of the Ramphastidae or family of toucans 1833–5 34 plates
(33 col.) J. & E. Gould del et lith 24 plates; E. Lear 9 plates; G. Scharf 1 uncol.
plate. Supplement 1855 21 plates J. Gould & H. C. Richter.
2nd ed 1852–4 52 plates (51 col.) J. Gould & H. C. Richter.

GOULD, J. A monograph of the Trogonidae, or family of trogons 1838 36 plates
Artists and lithographers: J. & E. Gould, (E. Lear assisted but no plate bears his
monogram).
2nd ed 1858–75 47 plates Artists and Lithographers: J. Gould & W. Hart; J.
Gould & H. C. Richter.

GOULD, J. Icones avium, or figures and descriptions of new and interesting species
of birds from various parts of the globe 1837–8 18 plates Artist and Lithographer
J. & E. Gould.

GOULD, J. A synopsis of the birds of Australia and the adjacent islands 1837–8
73 plates of heads of birds Artist & Lithographer E. Gould.

GOULD, J. The zoology of the voyage of H.M.S. Beagle 1832–36: volume III Birds
described by John Gould, with a notice of their habits and ranges, by Charles
Darwin, and with an anatomical appendix by T. C. Eyton 1838–41 50 plates
4to Artist & Lithographer J. & E. Gould.

GOULD, J. The birds of Australia 1840–48 7 vols. 600 plates Supplement 1851–69
81 plates Artists & Lithographers J. & E. Gould; H. C. Richter.

HINDS, R. B. The zoology of the voyage of H.M.S. Sulphur under the command of
Capt. Sir Edward Belcher during the years 1836–42; edited by R. B. Hinds
1843–46 2 vols. 85 plates Birds 2 parts 1843–44 16 plates (nos. 19–34) 4to Artist
& Lithographer; J. Gould & Benjamin Waterhouse Hawkins.

GOULD, J. A monograph of the Odontophorinae, or partridges of America 1844–50
32 plates Artist & Lithographer J. Gould & H. C. Richter.

GOULD, J. A monograph of the Trochilidae, or family of humming-birds 1849–61
5 vols. 360 plates Artist & Lithographer J. Gould & H. C. Richter.
Supplement (completed after Gould's death by R. B. Sharpe) 1880–7 5 parts 58
plates Artists: J. Gould and W. Hart; Lithographer: W. Hart.

GOULD, J. The birds of Asia (completed by R. B. Sharpe) 1850–83 7 vols. 530 plates
Artists & Lithographers: J. Gould & H. C. Richter; 34 plates J. Wolf & H. C.
Richter; Parts 33–35 (Feb 1882-Aug 1883) W. Hart.

GOULD, J. The birds of Great Britain 1862–73 5 vols. 367 plates Artists: J. Gould,
57 J. Wolf; Lithographers: H. C. Richter, W. Hart.

GOULD, J. The birds of New Guinea and the adjacent Papuan Islands, including
many new species recently discovered in Australia 1875–88 5 vols. (Parts 13–25
completed by R. B. Sharpe) 300 plates Artist and Lithographer J. Gould & W. Hart.

GOULD, J. A monograph of the Pittidae; edited by R. B. Sharpe 1880 One part
only issued with 10 plates from Birds of Asia, Birds of Australia and Birds of
New Guinea 7 plates Gould & Hart; 3 plates Gould & H. C. Richter; del et lith.

Additional books illustrated by Lear and Wolf—see under respective chapters.

JOHN GOULD

Additional books illustrated by W. Hart

BRITISH MUSEUM (Natural History) Catalogue of the birds in the collection...
1874–98 27 vols. 387 plates vol. XII 12 hand-col. autolithogs for Fringillidae by
R. B. Sharpe 1888.

DRESSER, H. E. A history of the birds of Europe including all the species inhabiting
the western Palaearctic region 1871–81 8 vols. 633 plates Colourer of many
hand-col. lithogs; lithographer of a few of J. Wolf's drawings.

ELLIOT, D. G. A monograph of the Pittidae, or family of ant-thrushes New York
1861–3 2nd ed London 1893–5 Artist for 2nd ed 51 plates.

SHARPE, R. B. Scientific results of the second Yarkand Mission, based upon the
collections and notes of the late Ferd. Stoliczka. Calcutta 1891 24 plates 3 hand-col.
autolithogs.

SHARPE, R. B. A monograph of the Paradiseidae, or birds of paradise and Ptilonorhynchidae, or bower-birds. 1891–8 2 vols. 79 plates 50 autolithogs hand-col.;
22 J. Gould & W. Hart del et lith hand-col. (from Gould's Birds of New Guinea);
7 J. G. Keulemans & W. Hart del et lith, hand-col.

SHELLEY, G. E. A monograph of the Nectariniidae (Cinnyridae) or family of sun
birds 1876–80 121 plates Colourer of hand-col. lithogs.

Additional illustrations by H. C. Richter

GRAY, G. R. The genera of birds, comprising their generic characters, a notice of
the habits of each genus and an extensive list of species 1837–49 3 vols. 335 plates
Artist 1 hand-col. lithog vol. I P1.XV Strix javanica;
Artist 1 monochrome lithog vol. I Pl.15 Head and claw of Phodilus badius and
Strix flammea
Artist 1 hand-col. lithog vol. 3 Francolinus clappertoni.

Zoological Society of London Proceedings 1848 Artist for the first two hand-col.
plates to be published in the Proceedings.

Caption for Plate facing page 48

J. & E. Gould's Narine Trogon (*Trogon narina* from Monograph of the Trogonidae,
1838 Pl. 26), is one of the brightly-coloured birds of which Gould was so fond. Elizabeth
Gould lithographed the designs, showing the pair of each species.

HENRY LEONARD MEYER

1798-1865

THOUGH the name of H. L. Meyer alone heads this chapter, the drawings and lithographs for his bird books were the concern of his whole family. In his family were his wife, formerly Mary Ann Moor of Woodbridge, whom he married in 1830, and their three sons and three daughters. In many respects Mrs Meyer was similar to Mrs Gould, for she not only helped with the sketches and drawings of the birds but was largely instrumental in their transfer onto the lithographic stones. The children, except for the youngest son Victor, appear to have done all the hand-colouring required for the finished prints of their second book.

Meyer was an Englishman of Dutch extraction. His father, an Amsterdam banker and elected Member for North Holland, came to England some time after Louis Napoleon established his kingdom in the Low Countries. Mr Meyer senior settled in this country, and died here. His son, Henry Leonard was an artist by profession and was also fond of natural history. He tells us in his Preface to *Illustrations of British Birds*, that "it has been the author's wish to represent the Birds as much as possible in their natural attitudes, for which purpose he had for some years past availed himself of every opportunity of studying them in Nature and had also kept a collection of living subjects, from which his drawings have been made as represented in the Quarto publication, now within a few parts of its completion".

This promises well, for there is hope of a new approach and more lively representations than those of Swainson and Gould. Nor are we disappointed upon opening the four folio volumes of *Illustrations of British Birds* (1835–41). These illustrations are very lovely lithographs of natural, life-like birds. The figures are very well drawn and the scrupulous work on the 313 plates has given us some of the most beautifully hand-coloured bird plates that have

59

been produced. The book was planned to come out in 79 monthly parts—a long and tedious project for them to have undertaken whilst trying to raise their family at the same time. In fact, the actual dates of publication of the parts are obscure, they were so erratic and irregular that they have defied the efforts of experts to establish the sequence and timing of their publication. The first part was issued in March 1835 and the last some time in the autumn of 1841.

To add to the confusion over when the parts were printed, they were re-issued several times, and the re-issues were in progress while the first edition was still coming out. Bound volumes of these parts vary in their number of plates and modern catalogues consequently quote different dates of publication and differing numbers of illustrations.

A series of 600 of Mr and Mrs Meyer's original drawings for the plates in this book are now in the McGill University Library in Montreal, Canada. Only one pencil sketch for the illustrations is in our national collection at the Natural History Museum, South Kensington. For these drawings, apart from birds in their own aviaries, Mrs Meyer used to visit the Zoological Society Gardens in London in order to sketch the birds there. Returning home, she would then draw the image, in reverse, on the stones.

No text was published with these *Illustrations*, but short notes at the foot of each plate gave such information as "$\frac{1}{2}$ natural size; Rare visitant; Food small animals; Nest placed in lofty trees; Eggs 2 or 3; In adult bird the belly is barred transversely with dark and light brown" in no more than three lines of letterpress. On each plate in the bottom right hand corner, is a picture of the species' egg.

Sometimes two birds were shown on one plate, occasionally only one member of the species. The feathering is not very detailed—a general impression of the bird being given rather than every line and feather being shown. The bird figures themselves are accurate and this coupled with the good colouring made the work attractive as well as being, at that time, the most reliable figures for identification purposes. With backgrounds they were not concerned, a branch being sufficient embellishment of the plate.

The work must have been a success for Meyer planned a second series, with a new title. It was to be published in bi-monthly parts this time, in conjunction with the parts of Yarrell's *History of British Birds*. It was an ambitious plan, considering their past record. A prospectus was inserted in the first part of Yarrell's book stating "The motive of the author in recommending the publication of the work at the time and in the manner specified is that it may appear before the public periodically with Mr Yarrell's History of British

H. L. Meyer

PURPLE HERON
Ardea Purpurea (Linn)
Adult and Young

Birds; which History, with the kind permission of that talented author, it is designed to illustrate in Colours—the representations of the Birds and other embellishments in Mr Yarrell's work being uncoloured. London June 1837''. Yarrell's work had many delightful wood engravings as text-figures. Meyer's idea was to supplement these with hand-coloured lithographs.

The almost inevitable result was that the parts after a very short time did not synchronise in their publication dates and soon became two entirely separate works. The Meyers' *Coloured Illustrations* were published in smaller octavo format. When completed, there were seven volumes, dated from 1842 to 1850, including 432 hand-coloured plates of which 102 were of eggs. Charles seems to have done most of the colouring and Constance Meyer is mentioned particularly as the colourer of the eggs. The drawings of the eggs were committed to Charles' care, he being a good artist like his parents. Charles was an ingenious member of the family. He invented a system of stencilling the colouring of the bird figures and the eggs, thus keeping the lines clean and also speeding up the tedious colouring process for his brothers and sisters. As before, the birds are all represented still and perched, usually with only a branch, with an occasional attempt at scenery in the background. The few backgrounds are very artificial compositions and would have been better omitted. The plates of eggs were inserted inter-alia as were some plates of details of claws, heads, etc. No juvenile birds were shown.

When the plan was altered, and the work was separated from Yarrell's publication, a text was added by Meyer, four or five pages of letterpress being given for each species.

Once again, there were so many issues and re-issues that they defy any dating and those whole editions of 1842–50 and 1853–7 contain a varying number of plates depending upon which copy is available for inspection. In the later issue the text is the same as that of the earlier edition, but some of the plates were redrawn and the colouring altered.

It was the practice at that time to produce a very small élite edition of a book, printed on special paper, usually of large size, for presentation to important people or high-ranking subscribers. Six copies of the second series of *Illustrations* were printed on paper measuring $22\frac{1}{4}'' \times 15''$ and carefully coloured for Queen Victoria, Prince Albert, Lord Middleton, the King of Holland, H. L. Meyer's own copy and a sixth copy which found its way into the Library at Welbeck Abbey. A few other, uncoloured, copies of this size have been traced, but for a "limited" edition this must take the prize for its very small number of copies.

The folio volumes were quite outstanding and of great value as an atlas of

British birds. At the time of publication they were in a class of their own. They were only bettered by Lord Lilford's *Coloured illustrations of the birds of the British Islands* published some fifty years later with chromolithographic plates. Lord Lilford recommended his artist Thorburn to look at Meyer's work, commenting (February 1887) "For very good accounts of habits and tolerable colour figures I should advise Meyer's British Birds in 7 volumes, but a good many new species and a great deal of new information have been brought to light since this book was published."

Another small book was published by Meyer in 1848 called *Game Birds and their localities*, with six hand-coloured plates. These were illustrations of "Grouse, Landrail, Woodcock, Snipe, Partridge, Pheasant" with a few lines of text for each bird. This is very rarely seen nowadays.

These publications have been largely forgotten due to their rarity and to their out-of-date text. Nevertheless, Meyer's books are worth more attention for the sheer beauty of their plates, the skill in the execution of the figures and careful hand painting. These can still be appreciated and valued today.

Bibliography

MEYER, H. L. Illustrations of British Birds. 1835–41 4 vols. with 313 plates, hand-coloured lithographs.

MEYER, H. L. Coloured illustrations of British birds and their eggs 1842–50 7 vols. with 432 plates (102 of eggs), hand-coloured lithographs.

MEYER, H. L. Game birds and their localities, accompanied by useful notes to sportsmen. c1848 with 6 plates, hand-coloured lithographs.

Caption for Plate facing page 60

Meyer's Purple Heron (*Ardea purpurea* from Illustrations of British Birds vol.II 1836 Pl. 4) the work of Henry and Mary, in the first folio atlas of British birds in which the life-size birds were lithographed and hand-coloured.

JOSEF WOLF

1820-1899

Wolf is an important figure in the history of ornithological illustration. He broke away from the domination of Gould's set bird tableaux by painting natural portraits of birds in motion. He achieved this without going to the other extreme, exhibited in some of the plates of Aububon. Technically his work is interesting, for his first book illustrations published in this country were reproduced by lithotints. He had a mild, though unhappy, flirtation with the early attempts at chromolithography, but above all he demonstrated the hand-coloured lithograph at its best. He was the author of many auto-lithographs and then later in his life ceased to draw on the stones and concentrated on being an animal and bird painter only.

Wolf was the first of a remarkably gifted group of Continental bird artists to settle in this country. Keulemans, Smit and Grönvold were all to follow in his footsteps and come to London in the second half of the 19th century, but Wolf was the pioneer animal painter to make England his home and find sufficient work to enable him to devote his whole career to drawing and painting zoological subjects.

Like many an artist, Wolf had a father with quite different aspirations for his son. Anton Wolf was Headman of Mörz in the district of Mayfeld near Coblenz, and farmed his own land. Josef, the eldest son, was born in the small village of Mörz on 21st January 1820. As a boy he loved to roam in the beautiful countryside near his home, observing the birds and flowers. He sketched and drew from living models, sometimes rearing birds at home for this purpose, but also occasionally shooting a specimen. Both birds and mammals were trapped and had their portraits painted. His village lay in the path of migrating birds of prey, which soon became his special favourites. He devised a spring trap in which to take these large birds without harming them. His father called him a bird-fool and was irritated by his lack of interest in the farm. It took Wolf some time to persuade his father to allow him to be apprenticed to a firm of lithographers in Coblenz. Lithography was then still a new process and it was a remarkable choice for a sixteen-year-old to make, but Josef had decided that this was the only way he could escape the farm and get some kind of start as an artist.

In 1836 he commenced his three-year apprenticeship with Gebrüder Becker and was soon given jobs where he could use his imagination and produce original flower, fruit and landscape designs. His drawings were improving and at the same time he was learning how to transfer them to the lithographic stones. When his apprenticeship ended, he returned to the farm for a year, during which time he made a collection of water-colour studies, in miniature, of a number of birds.

A visit to Frankfurt to see Dr Eduard Rüppell at the Museum there, in order to show him the paintings, was rewarded by a commission to do the illustrations for a book Rüppell was then in the process of writing about the birds of north-east Africa. Dr Rüppell also sent Wolf to see Dr Kaup, the Director of Darmstadt Museum. Wolf moved to Darmstadt and found work there as a lithographer, doing Dr Rüppell's drawings in his spare time. Dr Kaup took the miniatures to an ornithological conference in Leyden and an assistant at the Museum in that city, Dr Hermann Schlegel, promptly asked Wolf to execute some designs for the birds of prey for his *Traité de Fauconnerie*. Wolf had thus quickly become known to three of the most important European ornithologists of that period.

In 1840 Wolf moved to Leyden, and ceased working as a lithographer. From this time on he was a full-time animal and bird painter, only occasionally transferring his own designs onto the stones. He was still only twenty years old and in his work he had not yet developed his own free style. He was painting conventional, rather stiff, portraits with poor backgrounds, though his careful, conscientious attention to detail in his bird-figures made his illustrations superior to those of his contemporaries. Even when he transferred his own birds onto the stones, other artists were usually employed to supply the backgrounds. At this stage his work shows him to be more of a lithographic draughtsman than a fully-fledged artist.

He felt the need for more art training and attended an art school, investing some of his earnings in learning to draw and paint in oils. He began to take more interest in the background material, drawing trees and plants and observing how the animals and birds depended on these for camouflage, also how the plumage of the birds was related to their natural habitats. His

J. Wolf

RHINOCEROS HORNBILLS

Buceros Rhinoceros

realisation of the importance of the background in his paintings and his insistence on delineating every tiny mark on the plumage and the systematic arrangement of the feathers had its roots in this early training.

In 1846, for the first time, he was given free scope in the designs for some plates. These were for Kern the publisher. His preoccupation with the idea of presenting a dramatic incident or theme first took shape at this time. The earliest evidence was a picture of a fox springing at a capercaillie which flew off leaving the fox with a mouthful of tail-feathers. This interest in the battle in nature between aggressor and victim and the outwitting of the stronger creature by the weaker found expression repeatedly in Wolf's pictures.

For about a year, 1847–8, Wolf was at the Antwerp Academy, learning figure-painting. 1848, however, was a year of turmoil and war on the Continent and Wolf decided to leave the Academy. He did not wish to become a soldier, like his fellow-students, so went instead to London.

Wolf had a tenuous link with this country for Dr Kaup had visited London the previous year, praised Wolf's work when he met members of the British Museum staff and other scientists, and had interested John Gould in Wolf's drawings. Gould had asked Wolf for a small water-colour drawing of partridges, which had been duly sent. Wolf was invited to England on Dr Kaup's recommendation and was welcomed on arrival by D. W. Mitchell, the Secretary of the Zoological Society of London, and given temporary quarters in Fitzroy Square. He was also given room to work in the Insect Room at the British Museum and began work the very next day on the illustrations for Gray's *Genera of Birds*. George Robert Gray was a Fellow of the Zoological Society and Assistant in the Natural History Department of the British Museum. His influence in both these institutions was of great assistance in establishing Wolf as a member of the small circle of naturalists responsible for ornithological research in this country.

Wolf, whilst settling in and learning English, was also making other new friends among the scientists in the capital. There was Edward Bartlett, the Superintendent of the Zoological Gardens, and William Yarrell whom he met on an entomological outing, H. E. Dresser, a young man to whom Wolf took an immediate liking, and, of course, John Gould. Another friend, Sir Edwin Landseer, did Wolf a great kindness. He saw Wolf's picture "Woodcocks seeking shelter" at the Royal Academy and used his influence to ensure that it was hung in the 1849 exhibition. This was of tremendous importance to Wolf, for it meant that he had achieved recognition within a year of coming to England. It was also of financial benefit, as Wolf sold a large number of "woodcock pictures". During the rest of his life here, he was to exhibit another thirteen pictures at the Royal Academy and seven at the British Institution.

Wolf painted in both oils and water-colours, much of his work being sold to private collectors, and these originals are very scarce today. Ten portfolios of his original charcoal drawings, elephant folio size, and dating from the 1860s are in the McGill University Library at Montreal, but no sizeable collections remain in public libraries or museums in this country.

The elderly David W. Mitchell was engaged in doing the drawings for Gray's *Genera of Birds*, which had begun publication in 1837 and was now coming to a close. Mitchell had both drawn the designs and lithographed them, the printing being done by Hullmandel & Walton in Hullmandel's lithotints. Wolf was now given the task of helping Mitchell to complete the drawings and he was also expected to transfer them onto the stones. Wolf autolithographed eleven of the coloured plates and did a further fifty-nine monochrome plates showing details of the birds' heads, claws, beaks, etc. These detail plates included 345 heads alone, drawn by Wolf, and though his instructions were to produce merely scientific drawings, they are not purely draughtsman's work but have more artistic qualities. Wolf's work is easily distinguished from Mitchell's copies of the dead specimens from which they both worked. The lithotints are very lovely, with sensitive colouring and delicate tints. There is a pale blue wash or "tint" background against which the figures stand out clearly. More lithotints were printed in G. R. Gray's account of the birds brought home aboard H.M.S. Erebus & Terror after the epic voyage of 1839–43. Wolf contributed some drawings for this volume, including three of penguins, a small tern, an owl and an owl-parrot.

The Zoological Society, about this time, decided to include coloured plates in the printed record of their meetings and the papers read at them. The first two plates were done by H. C. Richter, then one by B. W. Hawkins preceded Wolf's first autolithograph in the *Proceedings* of 1849. This first plate illustrated a paper by G. R. Gray's brother, John Edward Gray, another officer at the British Museum, read on 8th September 1848, on a new genus of insectivorous mammalia. This was the first of some 330–340 plates, either autolithographs or designs of both birds and animals lithographed by others, which Wolf executed before 1865, after which he had so much other work that fewer of his plates appear in this periodical. His twenty-seven contributions to the *Transactions* of the Society were mainly mammal pictures. He also executed drawings for two other journals, *The Field* and *Illustrated London News*. Some of these original water-colour drawings, now much faded, are in the library of the Zoological Society.

JOSEF WOLF

Gould and Wolf worked together from 1849 in a cooperative, friendly manner, respecting one another's talents, though they were never really good friends. Gould had been a widower for eight years and had Richter to help him with the plates for his books, but was glad of the opportunity to enrol someone as good as Wolf to contribute additional designs. Wolf's scientific knowledge and ability to design pleasing groups and interesting attitudes were most welcome to Gould. Reproductions of some of Wolf's water-colours, drawn at this period, were to be included in Gould's first volume of *Birds of Great Britain*. This volume dealt with the birds of prey— the eagles, vultures, buzzards, hawks, falcons and owls—all of which Wolf thoroughly enjoyed painting. Gould was confident of Wolf's ability to produce excellent representations of these birds, having proof of this in the water-colour study which he owned of Wolf's Greenland Falcon, drawn for Schlegel & Wulverhorst's *Traité de Fauconnerie*.

Wolf maintained his independence and continued with free-lance work. He never liked being tied to one author or publisher. In fact, he never seems to have been committed to work for Gould in the way that Lear had been, and of which Lear complained that it brought him much misery. It is difficult to determine exactly what the relationship was. In Palmer's biography of Wolf there is an account of how Gould "acquired" the designs for Wolf's plates in the *Birds of Great Britain*. When Wolf went to see Gould at his house in Great Russell Street, he found a box of fourpenny cigars, to which he was addicted, waiting for him beside a large sheet of clean paper all ready and pinned to a board, with a piece of charcoal (for which Wolf also had a great fondness) conveniently to hand. Gould would no doubt wait for that moment of accord when their cigar smoke was gently curling upwards, then suggest, as a matter of friendship and not business, of course, that a drawing of a certain species would be welcome. This happened often enough for Gould to have a series of charcoal drawings, life-size, with a few additional water-colours, of 25 birds of prey, 14 ducks and 16 other species—no fewer than 55 in all—to include in his book. Gould may have commissioned, and paid for, some of the water-colour drawings. Either Wolf was no businessman, or else he was very soft-hearted. Perhaps he did not really mind doing the drawings, but he did object to the way the background was filled in by the lithographer and also to the over-colouring of the final print. Gould loved brightly-coloured birds and was not pleased when his plates were "dull" in his estimation. He liked all the birds of whatever species to be highly-coloured, and complained to Wolf about some of them, "There are sure to be some specimens brighter than we do them". Wolf always found greater pleasure in the subtle tones of the plumage of such apparently dull birds as the females of the partridges, pheasants and ducks. He was not as attracted to the brightly-plumaged birds as Gould.

In 1849 Wolf also contributed four autolithographs to A. E. Knox's *Ornithological Rambles in Sussex*. These included an osprey, a heron, a falcon with teal, and a plate with the title "Othello's occupation gone" indulging his love of the dramatic situation found in nature. He followed this up the next year with another quartet for the same author's *Game birds and Wildfowl*, in the same style. These eight autolithographs were tinted, but they are not very good examples either of Wolf's work or of the lithographic process.

The following year a better assignment came his way. David Mitchell was still kindly active on Wolf's behalf and introduced him to Lord Derby, the 13th Earl. Lord Derby was getting old, but his interest in the marvellous collection of animals and birds in his menagerie at Knowsley was unabated. Just as he had employed Edward Lear some twenty years before, so he now engaged Wolf to paint individual members of his collection. This was just one year before the Earl's death, and his aviaries then housed over twelve hundred birds representing more than three hundred species. There were also some three hundred and forty-five animals. If Wolf wished to see further specimens he could go to the museum at Knowsley which had twenty thousand specimens of quadrupeds, birds, eggs, reptiles and fishes. Wolf spent some two months at Knowsley and subsequently visited collections owned by other members of the aristocracy when they commissioned him to do drawings for them.

In 1852 the Zoological Society in London once again requested his services. The Council of the Society had agreed to an exciting plan to build up a series of original water-colour drawings of the most interesting subjects in their care. Wolf was the obvious choice amongst the artists then available, for who else could make excellent life-like pictures of both the animals and the birds in the zoo? The Society reproduced the first series of fifty drawings by folio lithographs, hand-coloured, with a short descriptive text added by D. W. Mitchell. These were issued in parts, commencing in 1856 and ending in 1861. There were many species on each plate, with scenes from the birds' natural habitats painted in the background. The plates were lithographed and coloured by J. Smit. Seventeen of them depicted birds, including a Greenland falcon and a "Mantchurian Crane". Before the completion of the publication of the first series, Mitchell died, and Wolf lost a kind friend and collaborator. Philip L. Sclater succeeded Mitchell as Secretary of the Zoological Society and took over the note-writing and preparation of the text for a second series of another fifty plates issued between 1861 and 1867. Smit was the lithographer and colourer of these, and this time there were twenty-two plates of birds. A rather nice saddle-billed stork, a shoe-billed stork and a gaunt Indian wood ibis formed part of this collection. Wolf had included many small chicks on his plate of the American rhea, though few of his other plates included young birds. Wolf had taken Smit under his wing when Smit arrived in England from Holland in 1866. Other lithographers besides Smit had done the work on the stones, copying Wolf's birds and animals and supplying the backgrounds. Wolf and Smit were on good terms and it is unlikely that the strictures made by Wolf on the lithographers concerned with this book included his friend. Wolf was rather upset about the backgrounds and when discussing the sky in one of the pictures which he thought looked very strange, he exclaimed, "And then they did the clouds, you see; one-two-three-four! They weren't even asked for that". However, despite the backgrounds, that hypercritical academic, Professor Newton, said of *Zoological Sketches*, "Though a comparatively small number of birds are figured in this magnificent work . . . these likenesses are so admirably executed as to place it in regard to ornithological portraiture, at the head of all others. There is not a plate that is unworthy of the greatest of all animal painters." (Article on ornithology in the 11th edn of Encyclopaedia Britannica). That was praise indeed. One particularly good plate is that of the great bustard, which is quite superb both in design, colour and execution. For many years the stones were kept and colour plates of these *Zoological Sketches* could be printed from them at the request of members of the public, who were charged seven and sixpence each for them.

1853 saw a great experiment in illustrating bird books. For the first time chromolithography was used to interpret an artist's bird-pictures, the designs having been drawn by Wolf. *The Poets of the Woods* appeared anonymously, published by Thomas Bosworth. From evidence elsewhere, it is now known that Joseph Cundall edited the selection of poems, several for each bird, which were illustrated by twelve small circular plates, cut out and mounted in gold borders. The small book ($9\frac{7}{8}'' \times 7''$) was bound in highly-fashionable emerald green cloth and is a charming period piece. The chromolithographic printing by the Hanharts is very good. Wolf allowed a further dozen drawings to be used in a companion volume the following year, called *Feathered Favourites*. The little song birds in these volumes are attractive and the chromolithographs are pretty, but do not suit Wolf's robust style. Wolf did not become involved in this kind of publishing again, but adhered strictly to serious scientific publications.

In 1856 Wolf took a working holiday in Scandinavia. He and Gould sailed on a private yacht for Christiana in Norway. Their main object was to investigate the breeding habits of fieldfares. They succeeded in this, and found many other interesting bird species. Many of Wolf's holidays were planned as bird-watching leisure periods. Among his other ornitholidays were a trip to the Bass Rock to see the gannets, and a three-day study of the birds of Handa. After watching the peregrines and sea-fowl all day he was taken off the island at night. Undeterred by the lack of binoculars (an innovation of the 20th century with regard to bird-watching), he took his Ross opera-glasses with him. Other breaks in his routine occurred in the summer of nearly every year when he returned home to see his family in Germany.

As more new species were discovered, bird-skins continued to flow into London and more rare birds to arrive at the zoo. Wolf was kept busy drawing them. From 1859 to 1869 he painted many such new birds for *Ibis*, among them some of the best of his drawings of raptores. In the course of these ten years Wolf contributed seventy-five drawings. In 1869 he was glad to relinquish this task to a newcomer, J. G. Keulemans, who had just arrived in England from Holland, where he, like Wolf, had been the protegé of Dr. H. Schlegel of Leyden.

The start of a new decade found Wolf moving house. He went to a studio with more spacious living-quarters in Berners Street, where there was ample space for him and all his pets. He filled his rooms with tame nightingales, whitethroats, chaffinches and many other small birds. His visitors made many new bird-acquaintances when they went to see Wolf. Charles Darwin sacrificed some white hairs from his beard when Wolf's favourite bullfinch joined the conversation piece.

We have already observed that Professor Alfred Newton approved of Wolf's work. He used two of Wolf's drawings in 1864 among the illustrations of his *Ootheca Wolleyana*. One was of an adult female gyrfalcon, which Newton claimed to be the only representation published in England at that time, and the other was of a golden eagle's eyrie showing young birds in the nest and a Scottish landscape background. Wolf had been on Black Mount near Glencoe in order to study golden eagles, and the painting used by Newton was a direct result of these observations. The two plates were reproduced by chromolithography. Another interesting link between Wolf and Newton, was a commission for a single drawing made by the newly formed British Ornithologists' Union. The head of the printing firm, Messrs. Taylor & Francis, in 1858 was Dr William Francis, and he had suggested that the journal of the Society be called *Ibis*. Wolf was asked to draw a figure of the sacred ibis. This figure, done at Newton's behest, adorned the cover of the first issue in January

1859, and is still used on the cover of each quarterly part to this day.

Most of the 1860s were taken up with drawings for the American author Daniel Giraud Elliot. Wolf's drawings were reproduced by hand-coloured lithographs in the two treatises published in New York, *Monograph of the Phasianidae* 1872 and *Monograph of the Paradiseidae* 1873. Wolf also did some of the designs for Elliot's *New and Heretofore unfigured species ...* 1869. Many more of his drawings of this period were translated into printed illustrations by the use of wood-engravings. These do not concern us here, suffice it to say that between 1853 and 1883 over three hundred of Wolf's drawings appeared as wood-engravings. It was also during the 1860s that parts of Gould's *Birds of Great Britain* (1862–73) were being issued, and many more hand-coloured lithographs after Wolf's drawings appeared in other natural history books.

Though containing only four of Wolf's plates, Stevenson's book *Birds of Norfolk* is interesting for it includes a scene of Scoulton Mere, the breeding place of the black-headed gulls, known locally as the Scoulton pewits or pies. Wolf drew a picture of the mere with clouds of gulls on the wing, also many birds both on the ground and in the water. The other three autolithographed plates are a capped petrel, a pair of hybrid duck then thought to be separate species and called Paget's pochard, and a pair of Pallas's sand grouse. These were printed in black or sepia.

The long-standing friendship with Dresser resulted in some fifteen designs of Wolf's being used in Dresser's *Birds of Europe*. This was published in eight volumes from 1871–81. Wolf's plates, published 1879, are of his favourite subjects—eleven birds of prey, two sand-grouse, and then a plate of a capped petrel. These drawings were done on a large scale in charcoal grey, with which Wolf preferred to work over and above any other medium. Dresser said of Wolf that he was at his best with the Raptores and understood their pose and characteristics better than any other. This was an opinion often repeated by Wolf's friends and subsequent critics.

In 1871 the painful chronic rheumatism from which Wolf suffered in the last years of his life first began to trouble him. Unfortunately, it affected his arm. We have very few bird plates from him after the 1870s though he continued to paint. In 1878 he had a very important commission for a painting of a pet bullfinch belonging to Queen Victoria. He was asked to paint it for a present to be given to the Queen on her birthday, the 24th May, by the Marquis of Lorne and Princess Louise. In this same year Wolf went to a new studio, at 2 Primrose Hill Studios, Fitzroy Road, Regents Park, so as to be near the Zoological Gardens where he was often to be seen sketching.

JOSEF WOLF

Gould's *Birds of Asia* in seven volumes had taken a very long time to produce, so long in fact that Gould died before the book was finished or the subject was exhausted. The last part was published posthumously in 1883, thirty-three years after the first plates had been issued. Wolf had done some plates for Gould in the early stages of the work and Richter had transferred eight of Wolf's birds of prey onto the stones for the first volume; a "Thibet Partridge" for volume six; and a further fifteen birds, all pheasants and partridges except plate 69 a mandarin duck for the seventh volume. One of the plates was done under strict instructions from Gould. This illustrated Heredotus' tale of the Egyptian plover cleaning a crocodile's mouth and shows the Nile in the background. No evidence of this behaviour has been seen by any reliable observer, and the crocodile has nicely spaced teeth unlikely to require such dental treatment, but Gould liked the story.

From this time on, we have no more book-plates from Wolf's drawings, though he continued to sketch both birds and animals. Still a bachelor, this kindly, benevolent gentleman with a large number of friends and admirers, died peacefully on 20th April 1899.

Wolf showed his birds in "suspended animation". They were always busy, getting on with their lives, and in the process of doing something. This habit of depicting a scene from a bird's life, not just a draughtsman's view of the bird's contours, marks Wolf out as a bird-artist of distinction. At the same time, his birds are carefully observed and are scientifically correct in every detail. He once complained that to naturalists he was an artist, and that artists regarded him as a naturalist. Where one or other of the two sides of his nature is allowed to dominate, his pictures are less satisfactory. His dramatic pieces are no longer to our taste, though the Victorians loved them. His early work, where every tiny feather and claw were immaculately drawn, lacked life and reality. Where he finds the balance, as in *Zoological Sketches*, he is at his best, but as he himself said, by that time he had learnt what to leave out as well as what to draw in.

Most artists are content to draw a typical member of a species. Wolf, and to some extent Lear before him, drew an individual member of each species. There is no trace of anthropomorphism, but the individual depicted has its own definite bird-character.

The artist and xylographer, Charles Whymper, another friend, said that Wolf was the first to make a full-time career of painting wild-life. He was only able to achieve this because of the scientific knowledge which was the basis of his art. This is confirmed by his own maxim, "We see distinctly only what we know thoroughly".

JOSEF WOLF

Another contemporary, Archibald Thorburn, whose favourite bird-subjects were the same as Wolf's, paid him this tribute, "Wolf's work is not only faultless as regards truth to nature, but there is, besides, an indescribable feeling of life and movement never attained by any other artist."

List of books illustrated by Wolf

DRESSER, H. E. A History of the birds of Europe, including all the species inhabiting the western Palaearctic region. 1871–81 8 vols. 633 plates Supp. 1895–6 89 plates Artist 15 hand-col. lithogs.

ELLIOT, D. G. A Monograph of the Tetraoninae or family of the grouse. New York 1865 27 plates Artist 1 hand-col. lithog.

ELLIOT, D. G. The new and heretofore unfigured species of the birds of North America. New York 1869 2 vols. 72 plates Artist for some of the hand-col. lithogs.

ELLIOT, D. G. A Monograph of the Phasianidae, or family of the pheasants. New York 1873 2 vols. 81 plates Artist 79 hand-col. lithogs.

ELLIOT, D. G. A Monograph of the Paradiseidae, or birds of paradise. New York 1873 37 plates Artist 37 hand-col. lithogs.

GOULD, J. The Birds of Asia 1850–83 7 vols. 530 plates Artist 24 hand-col. lithogs.

GOULD, J. The Birds of Great Britain 1862–73 5 vols. 367 plates Artist 55 hand-col. lithogs.

GRAY, G. R. The Genera of Birds, comprising their generic characters, a notice of the habits of each genus and an extensive list of species. 1837–49 3 vols. 335 plates (185 col.) Autolithographer 10 hand-col. and 59 monochrome lithogs, some Hullmandel's patent lithotints.

GRAY, G. R. & SHARPE, R. B. The Zoology of the voyage of H.M.S. Erebus and Terror under the command of Capt. Sir James Clark Ross during the years 1839–43; edited by John Richardson and John Edward Gray. Birds in vol. 1. by G. R. Gray 1844–5 37 plates (17 col.) Autolithographer of 6 signed plates.

Ibis volumes for 1859–69 mainly-few after 1869.

KNOX, A. E. Autumns on the Spey 1872 4 monochrome autolithogs.

KNOX, A. E. Game birds and wildfowl; their friends and their foes 1850 4 monochrome autolithogs.

KNOX, A. E. Ornithological rambles in Sussex 1849 4 monochrome autolithogs.

MOTLEY, J. & DILLWYN, L. L. Contributions to the natural history of Labuan and the adjacent coasts of Borneo. 1855 12 plates 5 hand-col. autolithogs – each plate showing many species.

RÜPPELL, W. P. E. S. Systematische Übersicht der Vögel Nord-Ost-Afrika's nebst Abbildung und Beschreibung von 50 theils unbekannten, theils noch nicht bildlich dargestellten Arten. Frankfurt 1845 50 plates hand-col. autolithogs.

SCHLEGEL, H. & WULVERHORST A. H. V. van Traité de Fauconnerie Leyden 1844 16 plates 12 hand-col. autolithogs.

JOSEF WOLF

SIEBOLD, P. F. von Fauna Japonica, sive descriptio animalium, quae in itinere per Japoniam...suscepto annis 1823–30 collegit, notis, observationibus et adumbrationibus illustravit. Aves Japonica; edited by C. J. Temminck and H. Schlegel 1844–50 20 autolithogs.

STEVENSON, H. & SOUTHWELL, T. The Birds of Norfolk, with remarks on their habits, migration and local distribution. 1866–90 3 vols. 8 plates-3 monochrome autolithogs, artist one monochrome plate lithographed by J. Jury.

SUSEMIHL, J. C. Abbildungen der Vögel Europas 1846–52 108 plates 11 autolithogs

WOLF, J. Feathered favourites: twelve coloured pictures of British birds 1854 Artist 12 chromolithogs.

WOLF, J. The Poets of the Woods: Twelve pictures of English song birds 1853 Artist 9 chromolithogs.

WOLF, J. Zoological sketches made for the Zoological Society of London from animals in the Regent's Park; edited with notes by D. W. Mitchell (and P. L. Sclater). 1856–67 2 series 100 plates Artist 39 hand-col. lithogs of birds.

WOLF, J. & FRISCH, F. Jagdstücke aus der hohen und niederen Jagd. Darmstadt (Ernst Kern) 1846 A number of autolithogs of game birds.

WOLLEY, J. Ootheca Wolleyana: an illustrated catalogue of the collection of birds' eggs, begun by the late John Wolley jun. and continued with additions by Alfred Newton. 1864–1907 2 vols. 38 plates Artist 2 chromolithogs (Plates F & G) in 1864.

ZOOLOGICAL SOCIETY. Proceedings, Transactions.

Caption for Plate facing page 64

Wolf's Rhinoceros Hornbills (*Buceros rhinoceros* from Zoological Sketches 1861 2nd series, Pl. XXX) were drawn from a living specimen in the Zoological Society Gardens, thought to be the only one in the country.

JOSEPH SMIT

1836-1929

J UST as Dr Hermann Schlegel (1804–1884, the Director of the Museum d'Histoire Naturelle des Pays-Bas at Leyden) had helped Wolf start his career by commissioning drawings from him for one of his books, so, twenty years later, he gave another young artist and lithographer his chance to become known and established as a bird-illustrator. Joseph Smit transferred all the drawings of Schlegel's illustrations on to the lithographic stones for *De Vogels van Nederlandsch Indie...* published in 1863–6 with fifty lithographs. Wolf had provided some drawings for Schlegel as well as doing lithographic work, but Smit was entrusted only with the lithography, and this difference right at the commencement of their careers was significant. Wolf soon abandoned the lithographic side of the work and became preeminently a bird-artist, whilst Smit never achieved this distinction but was usually employed as a draughtsman and lithographer, sometimes as a lithographer only.

Smit was a native of Holland, born at Lisse on 18th July 1836. Little is known of his early years, though he must, like Wolf, have taken a great deal of interest in the wild-life around him, and had some training as a lithographer. When he came to England he was already married and had a son, Pierre Jacques, who had been born at Leiderdorp in October 1863. Pierre was to follow in his father's footsteps and become an artist.

At the instigation of Philip Lutley Sclater, Smit came to England in 1866. In 1859, on the death of D. W. Mitchell, Sclater had become Secretary of the Zoological Society and was thus in a position to encourage, and give more substantial assistance to, young artists and scientists. Sclater was a keen ornithologist himself—dividing his time between his legal practice and natural history pursuits. His office in Hanover Square was a focal point for all the naturalists in London where they all found a welcome. Because of his special interest in birds, and by reason of his being an author who needed artists to illustrate his work, bird-artists were additionally welcome.

As soon as Smit arrived in England Sclater entrusted to him both the drawings and lithography for the illustrations to his *Exotic ornithology* which had descriptions and figures of new and rare American bird species. Sclater had a large collection of skins of American birds, which he had either collected himself on a visit to the U.S.A. in 1856 or purchased from other collectors. He and his close friend Osbert Salvin had prepared the text for this work and issued it in 13 parts between 1866 and 1869. There were 100 lithographs of Neotropical birds. Smit has done an excellent job with these plates, for the lovingly detailed birds stand out sharply against their backgrounds of trees, branches and leaves. It is obvious that Smit enjoyed painting the leaves as well as the birds, for they are beautifully executed. He also had a fondness for entwined, twisted branches which he sometimes showed wrapped round tree trunks or a larger branch. This motif occurs in a number of his pictures both in this book and later volumes.

Smit soon came in contact with Wolf who not only helped him by giving him work to do and recommending him to others, but also assisted him to settle in this country. Wolf gave Smit advice on domestic and business matters and, no doubt, a few hints on how to get on with the English. The two became very good friends and remained on excellent terms right up to the time of Wolf's death in 1899, having similar tastes and interests. The output of their work in the last quarter of the 19th century was considerable, and yet both have been largely forgotten. It might be truer to say that Wolf has been largely forgotten but Smit seems never to have been well-known. The reason may be that the much larger number of illustrations in bird-books executed by Keulemans in the same period has obscured the work of these two better artists.

At the same time as he was drawing from Sclater's American bird skins, Smit was busy with Wolf's water-colour sketches of the Zoological Society animals and birds for *Zoological Sketches* published 1861–7. This assignment suited Smit perfectly, for he was sympathetic towards Wolf's paintings, and just as Wolf could with equal facility portray both animals and birds, so was Smit similarly gifted, though not to the same degree as Wolf. No doubt by this time Wolf was so well established that he had sufficient work to allow him to concentrate on painting and he was glad to be rid of the labour of drawing the designs on the stones. He was fortunate to have found someone who could interpret his drawings successfully and it must have been a relief to pass this work on to Smit, as well as affording him some pleasure in being thus enabled to help Smit become established. P. L. Sclater also had a hand in this publication. He wrote the notes for the last few parts.

In the early 1870s Smit was engaged by **Dr. D. G. Elliott**, the eminent American ornithologist, to lithograph the drawings of a number of artists for his two monographs on the pheasants and birds of paradise. These were published in New York. Smit helped fellow-countryman Keulemans, then just arrived in England, to lithograph 81 plates of pheasants for the printers **M. & N. Hanhart** and **P. W. M. Trap** of Leyden. Smit also transferred all Wolf's drawings onto the stones for the 37 hand-coloured plates of Elliott's *Monograph of the Paradiseidae*, a series of highly coloured and exotic bird portraits.

Julius Lucius Brenchley (1816–73) a great naturalist and traveller, had been cruising on H.M.S. *Curacao* among the South Sea Islands in 1865 and found a number of fascinating birds. He wrote an account of the voyage from "jottings" he had made whilst at sea and handed the bird specimens over to G. R. Gray at the British Museum for their descriptions to be made out. When the account was published, only the birds new to science or particularly rare, which had been collected in the Western Pacific, were noted. The birds new to science were chosen to be depicted by J. Smit. He autolithographed the 21 hand-coloured plates showing single birds or pairs, with leaves and branches. One of the plates, of *Carpophaga brenchleyi*, shows a new species which Gray dedicated to Brenchley in 1870 in recognition of his services to ornithology. This scrub-fowl is now classified as *Megapodius eremita brenchleyi*, Brenchley's Megapode.

Another traveller, and a President of the Zoological Society, engaged Smit to draw some birds for him. Arthur Hay, 9th Marquis of Tweeddale, had reprinted from volume 9 of the *Transactions* of the Zoological Society "A list of birds known to inhabit the Philippine Archipelago". This was an attempt to list all the species of the Philippine avifauna. Smit did not draw portraits of all the 219 species then known, but was responsible for 11 plates. Smit's lithographs are bold and the birds drawn with swift, broad strokes. His larger birds are good and executed to give a general impression without much finicky detail. He shows some impatience with the foregrounds in these plates, most of the rocks, etc., being indistinctly drawn. In some cases, the white mark in the eye to give "life" to the bird is over-done.

When the Marquis' *Ornithological Works* were being edited for publication shortly after his death in 1881, some of the drawings Smit had already done for the *Transactions* and one from Rowley's *Ornithological Miscellany* were re-issued in this posthumous work.

JOSEPH SMIT

Lord Tweeddale was only one member of the aristocracy for whom Smit worked. At one time or another he drew animals and birds for the Duke of Bedford, Lord Rothschild, Lord Lilford and Sir Richard Owen, besides many other connoisseurs and collectors of water-colour drawings and sketches. These drawings remain in private hands and were never intended for book-work or publication. Only a few original drawings are available for inspection by the general public. In the British Museum (Natural History) are two water-colour drawings of cassowaries dated 1898 and three other birds, whilst a single, framed water-colour drawing of *Ara gossei* is kept at the Tring Zoological Museum.

Smit had many of his drawings published in periodicals. The Zoological Society quickly appreciated his conscientious, detailed work and printed his illustrations of animals and birds in their *Proceedings* and *Transactions*. For P. L. Sclater's paper "On the Curassows now or lately living in the Society's Gardens" published in the *Transactions* 1875–9 (9, IV and 10, XVI) Smit drew and lithographed the 21 plates. It is not possible to tell from Smit's plates which of these strange, ungainly birds with decorative knobs and crests were "now or lately living" for they are all life-like representations. Several issues of *Ibis* include plates after his drawings, many up to 1900 being autolithographs. After that date the three-colour process was used. Not only these scientific journals, but also more popular magazines used Smit's drawings e.g. *Nature* and *The Field*.

In the three years prior to his death in 1878, George Dawson Rowley, edited an *Ornithological Miscellany* to which many eminent authors of the day contributed articles on British birds and about birds of such remote places as New Zealand, Fiji, Mongolia, Northern Tibet, New Guinea, etc. Fourteen parts were issued, later bound into 3 volumes, with 135 plates. Most of the beautiful plates were after drawings by Keulemans and are highly-coloured. J. Smit contributed two plates to volume II with a variety of plates in volume III. Eight of Smit's plates of birds are in volume III as well as two more depicting large flocks of geese and an unusual illustration of bits of egg shell and gizzard stones. It is interesting to see Keulemans' and Smit's work in quite a different style in the large open country scenes. Neither of these artists is at all happy with such large vistas filled with flocks of birds in scale with their surroundings. Their normal work called for scientifically accurate delineation of bird-figures superimposed on small-scale background designs. It took an outstanding artist like Thorburn to produce convincing accurate portraits of birds in correct relation to their natural habitats. Thorburn also knew his birds in their natural state and was a field observer not a museum draughtsman. Keulemans and Smit failed in their attempt at this kind of work, as can be seen from these illustrations in Rowley.

Sclater, Brenchley and Lord Tweeddale had gone exploring on their own account and used their own private means to finance their expeditions. When H.M.S. *Challenger* set off in 1873 she carried a sponsored team of explorers and biologists for her journey of oceanic exploration round the world. The zoologist John Murray, later Sir John, was in charge of the work involved in recording and collecting specimens of the birds seen on the voyage. Some 903 skins were collected as well as some sea-birds preserved in salt and spirit. When the ship returned home in 1876 this material was distributed among several specialists to write up the reports on the different species. P. L. Sclater edited the "Report of the Birds collected...." in 166 pages in the volume on zoology published in 1881. The birds had come from the Philippine, Fiji and other Pacific Islands, Atlantic Islands and Antarctic America. Many eggs had also been gathered. The volume had 30 very fine reproductions of original drawings by Smit. These were collected together at the end of the book and are the usual Smit designs. The subjects included a number of penguins. On one of these plates (no. XXX) there is a delightful, if scruffy, chick of *Eudyptes chrysocome* accompanied by a more tidily-feathered parent bird. Smit's birds are invariably soft-plumaged and he manages to convey the feeling of the downy plumage most convincingly. His other birds are on branches with leaves, the latter, once again, showing evidence of careful painting.

Smit must have enjoyed doing the seven beautiful plates for that great character and distinguished cleric affectionately known to his friends either as the "Great Gun of Durham" or the "Sacred Ibis". Canon H. B. Tristram was a great traveller and collector and would disappear without any warning to his friends, to reappear some time later with new birds and stories of another adventurous journey either in north Africa, Palestine or elsewhere. He amassed an enormous collection of birds and eggs. Whilst in the Holy Land he discovered some ravens, which he deduced must be the descendants of the birds which fed Elijah and since the author of the Book of Kings had not given a clear scientific description of these birds, Tristram proceeded to make good this omission. He also gave them a new name, *Corvus Eliae*, after the prophet. On his return from one of these expeditions he wrote an account of the fauna and flora of Palestine, of which pp30–139 dealt with birds. Smit's seven hand-coloured lithographs were lively delineations of the rarest of the 348 species described by Tristram. One of these seven was a pair of Tristram's or Chestnut-winged Grackle (*Amydrus tristrami*). Another,

Plate VII, shows the White-throated Robin and is a typical Smit composition, with characteristic leaf detail and curling twig to accompany the charming portraits of the birds.

Much of Smit's time in the 1880s and 1890s, like that of a number of British ornithologists, was devoted to work on the *Catalogue of birds in the collection of the British Museum (Natural History)*. This immensely valuable treatise was edited by Dr. R. Bowdler Sharpe, an exceedingly industrious ornithologist who had succeeded Dr. G. R. Gray at the museum in 1872. Dr. Sharpe wrote fourteen of the twenty-seven volumes and edited the remainder. The 540 species chosen for the figures on the 387 plates had not previously been reproduced, or else not figured satisfactorily. When publication commenced in 1874 it was decided to have hand-coloured lithographs, but the amount of work this entailed was reduced when the editor changed to chromolithographs from volume XIV onwards. Smit joined in this great enterprise, contributing plates to volumes V, XVII, XIX, XXII, XXVI and XXVII along with J. G. Keulemans; doing all the plates in volumes VII, VIII, IX, XI, XIV, XV and XXVII himself; and being joined by his son to assist with volume XIII. Pierre had done the drawings for volume XVIII on his own. The sketches were not done entirely from specimens in the museum, but from birds in collections privately-owned as well. The compilers' aim was to include every bird known to science at the time of publication of each volume dealing with the group to which it belonged. Each of the volumes dealt with one or more groups of birds, with the appropriate plates collected at the end of the volume. Smit therefore found himself drawing members of such widely differing families as the *Gavidae*, the *Turdidae* and *Ramphastidae*. In those volumes for which he was responsible for all the drawings, he executed 88 plates, and when he shared the work with Keulemans or his son, another 30 or so plates. Each plate was signed "del. et lith." by the artist concerned and a note of the scale to which he had drawn the bird was given, as well as its scientific name. The birds were depicted on a branch with some foreground foliage, or on a stone, etc, but no backgrounds. Some plates had details of heads, these also being coloured, e.g. vol XIII Plate VII has four heads of the species of *Lamprocolius* drawn and lithographed by J. Smit. In the volumes where the illustrations were shared by Keulemans and Smit the two mens' different style is easily observed. Keulemans' work is crisper than that of Smit, the feather details being finer and the plants are also more detailed. Smit's birds are softer and given more lively attitudes, often shown balancing at more acute angles on their branches than the more sedate Keulemans' figures.

Smit

FIERY-BREASTED BUSH-SHRIKE

Laniarius poliochlamys

Another interesting comparison may be made in some of the other volumes of this *Catalogue*, this time between the illustrations executed by father and son. Pierre was esteemed as an artist, like his father. He had been drawing for many years before beginning his contribution to this series of volumes. He had sketched at the London Zoo, drawing small bird-pictures, whilst still a boy. These little pictures he sold to the public to help them identify the birds in the aviaries. After the few plates in volume XIII dealing with wood-swallows, starlings, weavers, larks, scrub-birds and lyrebirds, written by Sharpe and published in 1890, Pierre was allowed to do all the fifteen plates in volume XVIII devoted to the *Picidae* and written by Hargitt, published the same year. Pierre's woodpeckers have rather clearer lines than the birds drawn by his father, and they are shown in livelier attitudes, some flying, moving a wing, etc. He varies his style in drawing feathers, sometimes showing the rachis, vane and barbs clearly, at other times leaving the feather as a dark solid mass. Apart from a few plates for the third edition of Teget-meier's *Pheasants*, published in 1897 we hear no more of Pierre as a bird-artist. He appears to have found painting mammals, and more especially reptiles, more rewarding. He eventually left this country and died at Port Elizabeth, South Africa.

The last bird-drawings Joseph Smit did for a book were of specimens brought back from another scientific expedition. Dr. R. B. Sharpe dealt with the skins returned by the second Yarkand Mission from Central Asia in the ornithological section of the Report (published in 14 parts 1878–91). *Aves* were included in the last volume, some 350 forms being described but only 24 coloured plates were printed, two of these being done by Smit.

As he got older, Smit became more interested in animal portraiture than in drawing birds. When Wolf died in 1899, Smit was considered the best animal painter in this country, and from this time onwards drew more animals and fewer birds. He lived, full of vigour, to the ripe old age of 93, then died peacefully at his home in Cobden Hill in the little Hertfordshire village of Radlett.

Joseph Smit was a true disciple of Wolf, combining careful scientific delineation with life-like artistic representation of the individual of the species. He was more of a museum artist than Wolf, working largely from skins, being a good draughtsman for the purposes of ornithological indentifi-cation. This faithful reproduction of the many new species which he had to portray was exactly what was required by the scientists who employed him, but it precluded him from making a name as a bird artist with the general public. Also, he most probably knew that although similar to Wolf in so

JOSEPH SMIT

many ways, the older man was a better artist, both of animals and birds. Not as many of his designs were reproduced for book-work, consequently he is less well-known to ornithologists than he deserves.

List of books illustrated by J. Smit

BRENCHLEY, J. L. Jottings during the cruise of H.M.S. Curacao among the South Sea Islands in 1865. pp. 353–94 Birds, by G. R. Gray. 20 hand-col. autolithogs.

BRITISH MUSEUM (Natural History) Catalogue of the birds in the collection... 1874–98 27 vols. 387 plates Autolithographer of over 100 plates.

CORY, C. B. The beautiful and curious birds of the world 1880–3 20 plates artist 8 chromolithographs (published Boston).

ELLIOT, G. D. A Monograph of the Phasianidae or family of the pheasants 1870–2 2 vols. 81 plates (79 col.) lithographers: Smit and Keulemans for hand-col. lithogs.

ELLIOTT, D. G. A Monograph of the Paradiseidae or birds of paradise 1873 37 plates Artist J. Wolf, lithographer J. Smit.

ELLIOTT, D. G. A Monograph of the Bucerotidae or family of the hornbills 1876–82 60 plates artist 3 monochrome lithogs.

HAY, A. *9th Marquess of Tweeddale* The Ornithological works; edited and revised by R. C. W. Ramsay...1881 22 plates Artist 21 hand-col. lithogs.

LILFORD, T. L. P. *4th Baron* Coloured figures of the birds of the British Islands 1885–98 7 vols. 421 plates Lithographer of 1 Foster, 5 G. E. Lodge, 5 E. Neale & 6 A. Thorburn designs on 17 chromolithogs; 1 autolithog (Barred Woodpecker).

ROWLEY, G. D. Ornithological miscellany 1876–8 3 vols. 135 plates (104 col.) 13 autolithogs hand-col.

SCHEGEL, H. De Vogels van Nederlandsch Indie beschreven en afgebeeld 1863–66 3 vols. 50 plates Artist H. Schlegel; lithographer J. Smit.

SCLATER, P. L. On the Curassows, now or lately living in the Society's Gardens *in* Trans. Zool. Soc. 9, iv and 10, xvi 1875–9 21 plates hand-col. autolithogs.

SCLATER, P. L. & SALVIN, O. Exotic ornithology containing figures and descriptions of new or rare species of American birds 1866–9 100 plates hand-col. autolithogs.

SHARPE, R. B. Scientific results of the second Yarkand Mission based upon the collections and notes of the late Ferdinand Stoliczka 1891 24 plates 2 hand-col. autolithogs.

STEVENSON, H. & SOUTHWELL, T. The birds of Norfolk with remarks on their habits, migration and local distribution 1866–90. 3 vols. 8 plates 2 monochrome autolithogs (Pr of Great Bustards in vol. II; Feathers of wall-creeper in vol. III).

TRISTRAM, H. B. The survey of Western Palestine 1884 pp. 30–139 Aves 7 plates hand-col. lithogs.

JOSEPH SMIT

Zoological sketches made for the Zoological Society of London from animals in their
vivarium in the Regent's Park; edited with notes by D. W. Mitchell and P. L.
Sclater 1856–67 2 series 100 plates (of which 39 of birds) Artist J. Wolf; lithographer J. Smit.

Periodicals: Ibis
Zoological Society of London Proceedings
Zoological Society of London Transactions
The Field
Nature.

Caption for the Plate facing page 80

Smit's Fiery-breasted Bush-shrike (*Laniarius poliochlamys* from Catalogue of Birds
in the British Museum (Nat. Hist.) 1883 vol. VIII Pl. III) a hand-coloured autolithograph showing Smit's delicate work and care with soft feathering.

JOHN GERRARD
KEULEMANS

1842-1912

ANY author of a bird-book between 1870 and 1900 requiring an illustrator almost automatically thought first of Keulemans. This applied not only to English authors but many Continental writers too. Periodicals published in the same period had hundreds of his illustrations between their covers.

Keulemans was a Dutchman by birth. He was born on the 8th June 1842 at Rotterdam. As a boy he soon found his main interest was in natural history and that he had great facility in drawing various subjects which caught his attention in the field. The idea of combining these two interests in order to earn his living prompted him to take a job under Dr Schlegel at the Leyden Museum of Natural History when he was eighteen years old. Another of his enthusiasms made him resign the post two years later when he was given the opportunity to travel. Keulemans was always eager to visit other countries and during the course of his life he travelled across the length and breadth of Europe. He had a flair for learning languages and could speak five fluently. This first trip, however, was outside Europe. He went to Africa on a collecting trip. He also visited the Cape Verde Islands and the island of Principe off the west coast of Africa. He bought a coffee plantation on the west coast but was too ill with fever to continue living there and so returned to Europe and went back to the Leyden Museum. But Dr Schlegel did not retain the services of this artist and lithographer very long. For the third time in the course of a few years Dr Schlegel lost his protegé to London.

Dr Richard Bowdler Sharpe was responsible for Keulemans' coming to England in 1869. Dr Sharpe was five years younger than Keulemans but had already held the appointment of Librarian to the Zoological Society for two years. He had also issued some of the 15 parts of his *Monograph of the Kingfishers* and Keulemans had supplied him with the illustrations. Many of the specimens had been lent to Sharpe by John Gould when he first commenced work on the monograph in 1864. Obtaining the post at the Zoological Society Library enabled Sharpe to complete the book more quickly since he had easy access to so much material. Sharpe was obviously set for a great career as an ornithologist and author and he persuaded Keulemans to settle in England and illustrate his books for him. As can be seen from the bibliography at the end of this chapter the two men often worked together over the next three decades.

From the time he arrived in England, painting, drawing and lithographing birds became Keulemans' main pursuit. He lived for his work and devoted most of his time and energy to it. As a result, his output was prodigious. Of his private life he spoke little. Always a man of few words, deeply interested in spiritualism, very musical (being a talented performer on the 'cello, his favourite instrument), Keulemans was shy and unassuming. Most of his written work consisted of contributions to the subject of spiritualism, only two small books on birds being offered to the scientific world.

The first of his own books was issued in Leyden 1869–76 in 3 volumes with 200 lithographs executed by P. W. M. Trap after Keulemans' drawings. An attractive little book about cage birds was published in London two years after he settled there. It had 24 hand-coloured plates, some both drawn and lithographed by Keulemans, other drawings of his being placed on the stone by Trap. The book contains some foreign birds, e.g. a grey parrot; and some native British birds customarily caught and caged—finches, song-thrush; and rather more unusual subjects—nuthatch, bearded tit and magpie.

The plates in this last book, and in Sharpe's *Kingfishers* show Keulemans launched on his career with the plate "formula" which he was to use consistently and with very little variation, for all his subsequent work. One of the surprising factors about Keulemans' illustrations is that the last and first books he illustrated have the same type of illustration, and the intermediary plates are similar. He appears not to have greatly improved or changed his style during the course of all those forty years. Whether it was pressure of work that deprived him of the time to experiment or change, or whether he was satisfied with the interest inherent in changes in shape, size and physical make-up of the widely differing families of birds with which he had to deal, the fact remains that all Keulemans' plates look much alike in composition. Lest this sounds too severe a criticism, it must be stressed that his work was of a high standard, and, more remarkable, was consistently good. Hardly ever can one find a poor plate. Occasionally one can detect a careless finishing of foregrounds e.g. there are some rather poor tree trunks both in the Marshalls' *Capitonidae* and in *Biologia Centrali-Americana* and some haphazard scribblings—there is no other word for them—in the plates for Shelley's *Birds of Egypt*, but the bird figures are never below standard.

The formula devised for Keulemans' plates was based on the Gouldian pattern. A large bird species would be represented on the plate by one of the sexes only, smaller species by a pair. The figures would be set on a branch or rock and usually, though not always, shown at rest. Figures in flight, preening or stretching, etc. were the exception rather than the rule. Eggs, nests and juveniles might be included if specimens were easily available and the design of the overall picture permitted. The foreground would be fairly detailed, the middle ground a wash or tint and the background either tinted or, infrequently, a scene from the species' typical habitat. At the foot of the plate there would be Keulemans' monograph, JGK, written with a flourish, the scale to which the bird figure was drawn, and an indication of the sex of the bird figure.

The exceptions to this pattern are few, and therefore the more noticeable and interesting. Some of the game birds done for Baker had dense backgrounds and were quite a dark green with the bird figures painted to give a much more general impression than Keulemans' usual careful draughtsmanship allowed. A more solid background appears in the Australian bird plates for Mathews. These were done at the end of his life, whilst simpler backgrounds, or in some cases no backgrounds at all, were more usual in his earlier work. Many petrels done for Godman are among the liveliest of Keulemans' drawings—by virtue of their being shown in flight over water.

Another monograph of a bird family illustrated by Keulemans, was written by two brothers, G. F. L. and C. H. T. Marshall, who had served in the Bengal Army. They were attracted to the sturdy little barbets of the tropical forests. These birds are colourful, but very solid, stocky species with thick beaks, large heads and plump bodies. The *Monograph of the Capitonidae or Scansorial Barbets* included 73 lithographs done by Trap after Keulemans' drawings. Collecting together the specimens was quite a problem for these little birds are distributed in the tropical forests of most of the world. Keulemans had to use the collections of Lord Walden, T. C. Eyton, P. L. Sclater, O. Salvin, R. B. Sharpe and Alfred Wallace as well as public collections in museums. Many of the species were drawn and illustrated for the first time so Keulemans had to be very precise in his delineation. He devoted so much time and concentrated so hard on the birds that his foregrounds suffered in the process. This was an early work of Keulemans, and his foregrounds improved later, but these very poor tree trunks and branches and blurred foliage are some of the worst he ever produced.

Such a large proportion of the birds drawn by Keulemans were done from specimens that is is truly amazing that he could make the birds in his plates look life-like at all. He understood the anatomy of birds, also he was a keen bird-watcher, and these considerations obviously saved him from producing mere bird-contours in his drawings. It also, most probably, explains some of his apparent impatience with foreground and background material. Keulemans worked from skins, stuffed specimens, pickled specimens and some live models placed in the zoos and menageries around this country when collectors returned from expeditions all over the world. His period in London coincided with one of the busiest times ever known at the museums with hundreds of packages and cases of specimens arriving from Africa, the Americas and the East. Expeditions were leaving for the exploration of the oceans and their islands as well as the opening up of continents. There was plenty of work in depicting the highly coloured birds brought home from the tropics, sea-birds from ocean voyages, and a whole range of birds from all the different families for books about the avifauna of an island group or country. Great interest was being taken at this time in the closely related forms and species found in different parts of the world. These demanded very close and careful delineation to show the slight differences in size, plumage, thickness or length of bill, etc. These comparisons and studies were stimulated to a great extent by Darwin's theory of natural selection propounded in 1859.

Great credit is due to Keulemans that he could execute good drawings of many different kinds of birds. The highly colourful *Nectariniidae or Sunbirds* were sumptuously monographed by Shelley and painted by Keulemans. The feathering was highlighted in places by the application of what appears to be a clear varnish. In Shelley's *Birds of Egypt*, on the other hand, the plate of the pair of Egyptian nightjars (Plate VIII) shows the subtle tones of their cryptic plumage most beautifully executed. The sombre thrushes are also very attractively portrayed in Seebohm's *Turdidae*. Keulemans' versatility is best demonstrated in the avifaunas of countries which he illustrated and also in the large number of plates bearing his monogram in the British Museum *Catalogue of Birds*. Keulemans drew and lithographed all of the 121 plates in volumes I, IV, VI, X, XVI, XX, XXI, XXIII, XXIV which covered such diverse families as birds of prey, flycatchers, flower-peckers, wagtails, swallows, parrots, doves, rails, waders, etc. He also assisted J. Smit with the 88 plates of another six volumes and contributed a further four plates of finches to volume XII.

JOHN GERRARD KEULEMANS

Keulemans did a lot of work for Lord Rothschild who had his own private zoological museum at Tring in Hertfordshire. Lord Rothschild was very interested in the avifauna of Polynesia and the Malay Archipelago and had collectors in those areas. Their finds were sent back to Tring and reported in the museum journal *Novitates Zoologicae*. Keulemans drew a number of the new species obtained for Tring. Lord Rothschild's *Avifauna of Laysan* contained a complete list of the 116 forms of birds from the Hawaiian possessions. Keulemans provided most of the plates illustrating the birds with rather more background than usual and frequently included a young bird with the adult pair of a species. There are many of the original water-colour drawings for this book in the museum library at Tring. The hand-coloured lithographs are faithful reproductions of the original drawings, though the colouring of the prints is often brighter.

The birds in the first edition of Sir Walter L. Buller's avifauna of New Zealand are often quoted as being Keulemans' finest drawings. There were 36 plates, 35 of which were coloured by hand and reproduced from drawings of 70 figures. This book was limited to an edition of only 500 copies, which was twice as many as some of the limited editions of the period and explains why these scarce books change hands at such high prices today. Later editions of Buller had chromolithographs, but the supplement which was issued in 1905–6 had twelve additional hand-coloured plates. The highly-valuable first edition plates were hand-coloured by Dr. R. Bowdler Sharpe's three daughters, the Misses Dora Louise, Daisy Madeline and Sylvia Rosamund, with some copied from G. Edwards. Keulemans' background details of New Zealand flora were also coloured.

Many of the original water-colour drawings for Buller's New Zealand birds are in four beautifully bound volumes in the Zoological Museum at Tring. Some 35 of the sketches and drawings are in the McGill University Library, Montreal. Mr. Casey Wood states that these Canadian-owned sketches are of interest in showing Keulemans' method of working. We know that he often worked in pencil, from a comment by Dresser that Keulemans' "facile pencil has embellished so many works of ornithology". Mr. Casey Wood adds that he made sketches and wrote notes about the species to help him when he came to paint the water colour, or colour the lithograph by hand. Sometimes no water colour original exists where Keulemans drew his design directly onto the stone and then coloured the first print himself as guidance for the hand-colourers of further copies.

The majority of his drawings were reproduced by lithography, the plates then being coloured by hand. Of these quite a number were autolithographs,

J. G. Keulemans

BLUE-COLLARED LONG-TAILED SUNBIRD

Nectarinia metallica

though how Keulemans found time to both do the drawings and transfer them onto the stones is a mystery. Some of his best autolithographs are in Dresser's two monographs of the bee-eaters and rollers. Wolf gave up the effort of doing both as soon as he could, but Keulemans often did his own lithography. In the early part of his career here he would sometimes lithograph other artists' drawings. One outstanding example of this is the lithography for Elliot's *Monograph of the Phasianidae* where most of Wolf's 79 pheasant drawings were transferred by Keulemans who, as Elliot declared in the prospectus for his book (*Ibis* 1869) "is fast establishing himself as a first-rate draughtsman of animal life".

Only four titles to which Keulemans contributed drawings have plates produced by chromolithography. The *Catalogue* of the British Museum birds already mentioned used this process from volume XIV onwards. Dr. Sharpe, editor of the *Catalogue*, also edited Allen's Naturalist's Library and wrote four volumes in the series entitled *A Handbook of the Birds of Great Britain*. These volumes have some very interesting plates. Most of the figures are reprinted outlines of the engraved plates from Jardine's *Birds of Great Britain and Ireland* (1839–43) overprinted with colour lithography. Keulemans contributed a few additional plates e.g. vol iv plates CXIa to CXXIII and the frontispiece XCIV which are all in pure chromolithography. The illustrations in the two volumes on *Game-birds* by Ogilvie-Grant in the same series are similarly of mixed origin, with some plates from the earlier *Game-birds* 1834–43 by Sir William Jardine overprinted with colour, and a few chromolithographs by Keulemans. The third title is Lilford's *Coloured figures* for which Keulemans worked on 125 chromolithographed plates in the earlier volumes until he became ill and ceased work for a while. This was in 1887, when Thorburn took over the work for Lord Lilford.

Keulemans occasionally let others lithograph his designs. Hart lithographed seven birds of paradise and bower-birds for Shelley's monograph and Smit transferred a number of his drawings for Rowley's *Ornithological Miscellany*. Most of the 104 hand-coloured plates for Rowley were after sketches by Keulemans but they were not at all his usual type of bird-illustration. Some unique scenes are included in this work e.g. 'Mother Carey and her Chickens' shows a witch on a broomstick and *Thalassidroma Bullockii* or Bullock's Petrel. Another plate is of feathers only. This miscellany is a fascinating pot-pourri and a number of artists must have been surprised at finding themselves painting strange scenes and curious objects for the illustrations. Keulemans contributed hundreds of drawings for the plates in more conventional ornithological magazines. His drawings were included in the Hun-

JOHN GERRARD KEULEMANS

garian Journal *Aquila* and the German *Journal für Ornithologie*. At home, the *Quarterly Magazine* of the High Wycombe Natural History Society edition 1866–7 had printed one of his first plates, for Sharpe's paper on the crested kingfishers of Africa. In 1869 Keulemans took Wolf's place in the *Ibis*, working on its illustrations until 1909. The Zoological Society also printed a large number of plates signed 'JGK' in its *Proceedings* and *Transactions*—many of these being illustrations of species new to science, others careful details of heads and other parts of birds. Lord Rothschild's *Novitates Zoologicae* had many beautiful plates by the two artists Grönvold and Keulemans, though the latter contributed more over the period 1894–1910.

The great value of Keulemans' work as an ornithological draughtsman lay in his sureness of design of the plate and his accuracy in portraying the birds themselves. The bird figures were carefully drawn and executed down to the last scales on the feet. The feathering was neatly delineated with the different plumes receiving sympathetic treatment, the fine soft under-plumage and the large flight feathers being equally well drawn. Keulemans had not the imagination of Wolf and did not attempt to show his birds in more than a few basic attitudes—most of the figures being firmly perched on rocks or branches. His work appears a little austere as a result and lacks the charm of many of Thorburn's plates or the vitality of Wolf's paintings. As an ornithological draughtsman, purely and simply, however, he was outstanding.

Keulemans died in 1912 before the first world war virtually put an end to his type of book illustration work. Those artists who lived through the war found that the era of fine hand-coloured, or chromolithographed, folio plates illustrating bird-books had been brought to a close. This sad change Keulemans had been spared. He lived the last few years of his life by the sea at Southend. He was married twice and left nine children.

List of books illustrated by Keulemans

Aquila

BAKER, E. C. S. The Indian ducks and their allies 1908 30 plates Artist for 10 hand-col. lithogs.

BAKER, E. C. S. Game birds of India 1921–30 3 vols. 75 plates (60 col.) Artist for 7 hand-col. lithogs in vol. I.

BLAAUW, F. E. A Monograph of the Cranes 1897 22 plates 7 hand-col. autolithogs; lithographer 15 hand-col. lithogs after drawings by H. Leutemann.

90

JOHN GERRARD KEULEMANS

BLANFORD, W. T. Observations on the geology and zoology of Abyssinia 1870 12 plates 6 hand-col. autolithogs.

BRITISH MUSEUM (Natural History) Catalogue of the birds in the collection... 1874–98 27 vols. 387 plates Artist and lithographer for over 160 hand-col. lithogs and chromolithogs.

BULLER, Sir W. L. A History of the birds of New Zealand 1873 36 plates (35 col.) artist for 35 hand-col. lithogs (2nd ed 1888 chromolithogs) Supp. 1905–06 2 vols. 17 plates Artist hand-col. lithogs.

CRAWSHAY, R. The birds of Tierra del Fuego 1907 44 plates (21 col.) Artist 21 hand-col. lithogs.

DRESSER, H. E. A History of the birds of Europe including all the species inhabiting the western Palaearctic Region 1871–81 8 vols. 633 plates Chief artist for hand-col. lithogs; Supplement 1895–6 89 plates Artist for 84 hand-col. lithogs.

DRESSER, H. E. A Monograph of the Meropidae, or family of bee-eaters 1884–6 34 plates hand-col. autolithogs.

DRESSER, H. E. A Monograph of the Coraciidae, or family of the rollers 1893 27 plates hand-col. autolithogs.

ELLIOT, D. G. A Monograph of the Bucerotidae, or family of the hornbills 1876–82 60 plates Artist 57 hand-col. lithogs.

GODMAN, F. du C. A Monograph of the petrels (order Tubinares) 1907–10 2 vols. 106 plates Artist 103 hand-col. lithogs.

HAY, A. Ornithological works 1881 22 plates artist 1 hand-col. lithog.

Ibis 1869–1909

Journal Für Ornithologie

KEULEMANS, J. G. Onze Vogel in huis en tuin, beschreven en afgebeeld 1869–76 3 vols. 200 plates Artist hand-col. lithogs.

KEULEMANS, J. G. A Natural history of cage birds 1871 24 plates hand-col. autolithogs.

LAYARD, E. L. The Birds of South Africa 2nd ed 1875–84 12 plates Artist hand-col. lithogs.

LEGGE, W. V. A History of the birds of Ceylon 1880 36 plates hand-col. autolithogs.

LILFORD, T. L. P. 4th Baron Coloured figures of the birds of the British Islands 1885–98 7 vols. 421 plates Artist 125 chromolithogs.

MARSHALL, G. E. L. and MARSHALL, C. H. T. A Monograph of the Capitonidae or scansorial barbets 1870–71 73 plates Artist hand-col. lithogs.

MATHEWS, G. M. The Birds of Australia 1910–27 12 vols. 600 plates Artist 163 hand-col. lithogs in vols. 1–3.

MATHEWS, G. M. The Birds of Norfolk and Lord Howe Islands and the Australasian South Polar Quadrant 1928 45 plates (38 col.); Supp. 1936 57 plates (40 col.) Artist 1 hand-col. lithog (Plate 90 White-fronted fantail).

MITCHELL, F. S. The Birds of Lancashire 1885 11 plates Artist 2 hand-col. lithogs Novitates Zoologicae 1894–1910.

OGILVIE-GRANT, W. R. A Handbook to the game birds (Allen's Naturalist's Library) 1895–7 2 vols. 42 plates Artist for a few chromolithogs.

ROTHSCHILD, L. W. *2nd Baron* The Avifauna of Laysan and the neighbouring islands 1893–1900 83 plates (52 col.) Artist for about 40 hand-col. lithogs.

ROWLEY, G. D. Ornithological miscellany 1876–8 3 vols. 135 plates (104 col.) Artist 89 hand-col. lithogs birds and eggs.

SALVIN, I. & GODMAN, F. du C. Biologia Centrali-Americana; Aves 1879–1904 4 vols. 84 plates Artist 82 hand-col. lithogs.

SCHLEGEL, H. & POLLEN, F. P. L. Recherches sur la Faune de Madagascar...: Mammifères et Oiseaux, 1868 40 plates (38 col.) Artist H. Schlegel; Lithographer Keulemans.

SCLATER, P. L. A Monograph of the jacamars and puff-birds or families of Galbulidae and Bucconidae 1879–82 55 plates hand-col. autolithogs.

SCLATER, P. L. & HUDSON, W. H. Argentine ornithology 1888–9 2 vols. 20 plates hand-col. autolithogs.

SEEBOHM, H. The Geographical distribution of the family Charadriidae, or the plovers, sandpipers, snipes and their allies 1887–8 21 plates Artist hand-col. lithogs.

SEEBOHM, H. Monograph of the Turdidae, or family of thrushes 1898–1902 2 vols. 149 plates hand-col. autolithogs.

SHARPE, R. B. Report on the second Yarkand Mission 1878–91; Aves 1891 24 plates 15 hand-col. autolithogs.

SHARPE, R. B. A Chapter on birds; rare British visitors 1895 18 plates Artist chromolithogs.

SHARPE, R. B. A Hand-book to the birds of Great Britain (Allen's Naturalist's Library) 1894–7 4 vols. 128 plates Artist for 14 chromolithogs in vol. IV.

SHARPE, R. B. A Monograph of the Alcedinidae or family of kingfishers 1868–71 121 plates Artist hand-col. lithogs.

SHARPE, R. B. A Monograph of the Paradiseidae, or birds of Paradise and Ptilonorhynchidae, or bower-birds 1891–8 2 vols. 79 plates artist 7 hand-col. lithogs.

SHELLEY, G. E. A Handbook to the birds of Egypt 1872 14 plates Artist hand-col. lithogs.

SHELLEY, G. E. A Monograph of the Nectariniidae (Cinnyridae) or family of sunbirds 1876–80 121 plates hand-col. autolithogs.

ZOOLOGICAL SOCIETY OF LONDON Proceedings, Transactions.

Caption for Plate facing page 88

Keulemans' Blue-collared Long-tailed Sunbird (*Nectarinia metallica* from G. E. Shelley's Handbook to the Birds of Egypt 1872 Pl. IV), a rare lithograph (hand-coloured) of a bird in flight, otherwise his usual plate composition.

EDWARD NEALE

flourishing c.1870-1890

EDWARD NEALE was a Victorian bird-artist of some talent. He worked for only five authors with fewer than two hundred of his drawings being reproduced by lithographic means for books about birds. This partly accounts for his being relatively unknown and he is certainly without sufficient honour. During recent years his work has become more esteemed, largely due to a return to favour of Victorian artists and a renewed interest in prints from their drawings. Neale also suffers from our having no knowledge of his background, training, residence, or any other personal detail which would enable us to form some idea of his personality.

Most of Neale's work was concerned with European and British bird species, and much less with the avifauna of other countries. He contributed two plates to the bird section of Salvin and Godman's account of the fauna of Central America, working from specimens brought back from the authors' expeditions to that large region. Both of these plates are of birds of prey. He painted ducks, partridges and pheasants for Hume and Marshall's *Game birds of India*. This book had one hundred and forty-four chromolithographs for which Neale and Foster were the main artists. Neale's work is much more detailed, natural and generally workmanlike than that of Foster. Though there are a great many blurred backgrounds in these plates, those of Neale are clearer and crisper. His contributions were bird figures true to life but not life-like. The colouring of the chromolithographs is poor.

H. E. Dresser asked Neale to do some drawings for his *Birds of Europe*. Dresser was a businessman by profession and an amateur bird-watcher and collector. He took every opportunity to travel abroad and collected eggs and bird-skins with tremendous enthusiasm. He eventually amassed a collection of twelve thousand bird skins which were donated to Manchester University.

93

EDWARD NEALE

He commenced work on his *Birds of Europe* in 1871, with the cooperation of Dr R. B. Sharpe. After part xii had been issued, Dr Sharpe had to leave Dresser to finish the book by himself, as he had more than enough work to do in his new post at the British Museum. Dresser's text is highly scientific, his aim being to give a comprehensive account of all the European birds. Each species mentioned in the text was illustrated. Neale, and the other illustrators, used Dresser's large collection of skins for their drawings. The plates have a uniform layout and content. The usual "Gouldian" formula is followed, with most birds perched either on a branch or on the ground, fairly detailed foreground plants and terrain, a lightly sketched background, pale blue tinted sky. As to the birds themselves, there is usually one per page for the larger species, two where it is necessary to show the difference in plumage between male and female, and an occasional chick or immature bird. No eggs are depicted as Dresser planned a further book devoted entirely to European birds' eggs. The plates were printed by M & N Hanhart, some by T. Walter, and others by Mintern Brothers, then hand-coloured by W. Hart and a "Mr Smith". The book was originally issued in eighty-four parts at twelve shillings each part, which was far from cheap.

Keulemans did most of the plates for Dresser, with a few contributions from Wolf, Neale and Thorburn. Neale was responsible for a number of drawings of rails and crakes in volume 7, as well as the "Caspican" and "Caucasian Snow" Partridges. In volume 8 there is a delightful study of four ruffs in the full splendour of their breeding plumage, the following plate depicting the reeve with two chicks. There are many little chicks in this work and Neale has provided examples of the young of the water-rail, among others. He also autolithographed some birds of prey e.g. in volume 5 the lesser and larger spotted eagles. Occasionally he is noted as the lithographer of other artists' work. He lithographed Wolf's pallid and Montagu's harriers. His foregrounds are far more detailed and carefully executed than those of Keulemans. Both artists clearly outlined all the feathers but did not fill in the detail. Neale did not paint birds' eyes very well. He achieved a "staring" effect, rather as though he had painted glass eyes, a result no doubt of working from stuffed specimens supplied with that very commodity.

Neale contributed six drawings for Lord Lilford's *Coloured figures*. His picture of a red grouse was lithographed by J. Smit and then printed, but Lord Lilford suppressed it as not being up to standard and it was replaced by a print after a drawing by Thorburn. The five plates using Neale's drawings were all lithographed by Smit; the birds being black grouse, common partridge and a ptarmigan in its autumn, summer and winter plumage which occupied three plates. Neale's plates were issued September and December 1888 in parts vii and viii. This was the period when Keulemans was ill and Lord Lilford was trying to find other illustrators. Thorburn was submitting his first drawings about the same time and was to become the chief illustrator in Keulemans' place.

Neale's most important assignment was given him by Edward T. Booth. This bird-watcher was a very wealthy man and could indulge himself full-time in his hobby. With his gun in hand he stalked the marshes near Rye, then the Norfolk Broads, and finally went further afield to the Highlands and Lowlands of Scotland, in search of birds. From a gentleman who combined the two jobs of cutting men's hair and stuffing birds, Booth learned the art of taxidermy and proceeded to stuff all his own birds and set them up in glass cases. The cases were fitted up to represent the birds in their natural surroundings. These came into the possession of the Brighton townspeople at Booth's death in 1890. Many of these specimens, now in the Brighton Museum, were figured by Neale in *Rough Notes*. Neale provided the drawings for all of the one hundred and fourteen hand-coloured lithographs and this time we have evidence of his work on other species than game birds and birds of prey. These are very handsome folio plates whose composition is similar to those in Dresser's book. The first plate is of a golden eagle. Neale was famous for a splendid oil painting of this species, the canvas measuring three feet by two feet and four inches. Unfortunately we cannot compare this with the plate in Booth's book, for the unfinished oil painting is now in Montreal. There are no original Neale paintings in our national collections. On the plates Neale has placed either a single bird, a pair of birds, or a pair with chicks. He is careful to note, at the foot of the plate, the age of the birds in their different plumage, Booth's work being a study of this aspect of the subject. The chicks are very good, with the exception of some rather scruffy-looking crested tits. Neale was not capable of drawing soft plumage satisfactorily, though he came nearer to conveying a sense of softness with the chicks. He used rather hard lines to divide the plumage in the areas between one kind of feathering and another, and also between different colours. Some of the colouring was imprecisely applied by hand and was not always accurate e.g. the bearded tits are over-coloured. His birds do not fly, bathe, walk or preen, but just sit still on their perches as neatly and unruffled as they did in Booth's glass cases.

These titles include all the lithographs after Neale's drawings but they were not the only bird books illustrated by him. A large number of his drawings were copied by wood-engravers.

EDWARD NEALE

Neale was handicapped by working always from mounted specimens or skins. Perhaps he had little time to bird-watch, or little inclination, but his work suffers from this lack of knowledge of the living models. He was a competent draughtsman, but his work does not rise above that limit and he cannot be regarded as a first-rate bird-artist.

Books illustrated with lithographs after Neale's drawings

BOOTH, E. T. Rough notes on the birds observed during 25 years' shooting and collecting in the British Islands 1881–87 3 vols. 114 plates hand-col. autolithogs.

DRESSER, H. E. A History of the birds of Europe including all the species inhabiting the western Palaearctic region 1871–8 18 vols. 633 plates Artist for a few hand-col. lithogs.

HUME, A. O. & MARSHALL, C. H. T. Game birds of India, Burma and Ceylon 1879–81 3 vols. 144 plates Artist 44 chromolithogs (some plates reprinted in FINN, F. Indian sporting birds 1913).

LILFORD, T. L. P. *4th Baron* Coloured figures of the birds of the British Islands 1885–98 7 vols. 421 plates Artist for five chromolithogs.

SALVIN, O. & GODMAN, F. du C. Biologia Centrali-Americana: Aves 1879–1904 4 vols. 84 plates Artist 2 hand-col. lithogs (Plates 62, 66).

Caption for Plate facing page 96

Neale's Ruffs (*Machetes pugnax*, from Dresser's History of Birds of Europe 1881 vol. 8, Pl. 557) is one of the most attractive of all his plates, and perhaps the liveliest. He drew the design for the hand-coloured lithograph.

RUFFS

Machetes pugnax

E. Neale

W. Foster

GREY-BELLIED TRAGOPAN
Ceriornis blythii

WILLIAM FOSTER

1852-1924

WILLIAM FOSTER was the son of a very famous father. Much has been written about Myles Birket Foster (1825–1899) whose drawings of scenes of Venice, Brittany and the Rhine are greatly prized by collectors today, but very little information is available about his son. Birket Foster also made charming little vignettes after the style of his friend Bewick, for engravings to be used to illustrate poetry books. His second son, William, born on the 6th January 1852 at Carlton Hill, London, inherited his father's varied abilities to a degree, but was never as famous. No doubt, he also was influenced by Bewick's work and the wood-engraver's love of natural history, particularly birds.

One advantage in being the son of an artist was that William's wish to draw and paint was encouraged. After being educated at Guildford Grammar School, he was sent to Heatherley's to study painting. He succeeded in exhibiting his paintings at the Royal Academy, at Suffolk Street, and the Institute, but he became better known as a book illustrator. Much of his work was reproduced in children's books and volumes on natural history subjects. He was a member of the Water-colour Society from 1870, his painting being done chiefly at Witley, in Surrey, where his father had taken the family to live in 1858.

Dr R. B. Sharpe proposed Foster's election as a member of the British Ornithologists' Union in 1880, the year in which his illustrations of Indian birds were appearing in the parts of Hume & Marshall's *Game birds of India*. This was the only ornithological work of importance to include a number of plates from his drawings.

Allan Octavian Hume (1829–1912) held several high posts in India and collected a large museum of birds, and their eggs, at Simla. He cooperated with a colonel in the Indian army, Charles Henry Tilson Marshall (1841–1927), in producing a text on the game birds of India, Ceylon and Burma. The three volumes were published between 1879 and 1881 in a very small edition for subscribers only. The one hundred and forty-four chromolithographs were from drawings by many artists. M. Herbert, A. W. Strutt, S. Wilson, and C. J. Davenport all contributed, but Edward Neale and William Foster did most of the illustrations. The first volume dealt with bustards, florican, pheasants, peafowl, jungle and spur-fowl, for which Foster did ten plates, including three gaudy tragopans, three of the colourful spur-fowl and two snow-cocks. Each one of his dozen plates in volume II were of partridges, and these with the other members of the order Galliformes in volume I were colourful drawings of these highly patterned birds. Foster's style and approach was dissimilar in many ways from that of his fellow-artists. He utilised the full page, filling it with background details, much foreground vegetation, with a pair of bird figures superimposed. In the third volume of *Game birds* Foster did the drawings for thirty-three plates depicting ducks, geese and swans. Though in the same style, these are a little lighter in tone, some of them being less cluttered with background details. Neale's plates, by contrast, are much lighter, clearer and crisper. Foster attempted to give a general impression of the birds, not a detailed feather-by-feather account of their appearance. He fills in coloured areas rather than carefully painting each feature. The figures themselves are a little stiff, some of them having un-natural attitudes or postures. Too often, the white eye-mark is carelessly applied. The whole result is not so much a feeling of a more natural, spon-taneous picture of the bird, but, regrettably, of not sufficiently careful painting. Some of the fault might well lie with the poor chromolithographic printing, and the colouring and lithography of T. Walter.

Only one of Foster's drawings for Lord Lilford was published and included in *Coloured figures*. This was a figure of a woodcock, lithographed by J. Smit, for part vii, issued in September 1888. Foster also did a drawing of a nightjar, which was lithographed by Smit and printed by Mintern Bros., but Lord Lilford considered it unsatisfactory and suppressed it.

Foster had a very long illness before he died on the 24th May 1924, in London. During his last years he had been at work on a set of careful studies of British birds, in water-colours. For many species he had made a complete record of the bird, from the egg through the various plumage stages to the adult bird. He finished five hundred and sixty-two of these water-colour paintings. Many of the birds had been drawn from life, either in the field or when Foster visited the Zoological Gardens in Regent's Park, though for the rarer species he had had to resort to the specimens in the Natural History Museum, South Kensington.

This shy, retiring, artist also did some illustrations for C. A. John's *British birds in their haunts*, a book which went through many reprints and editions. First published in 1862, it had contained some charming wood-engravings by Charles and Josiah Whymper after drawings by Wolf. For the new edition of 1907, by J. A. Owen, Foster did some paintings for sixty-four coloured plates. These were reproduced photographically.

It is a pity that Foster's drawings have not been well reproduced. We have so few plates by which to judge his work, that we are unable to form a true opinion of his abilities as a bird illustrator. His qualities as a bird artist are higher than the plates made from his drawings would suggest.

Books containing chromolithographs after drawings by Foster

HUME, A. O. & MARSHALL, C. H. T. Game birds of India, Burma, and Ceylon. 1879–1881 144 plates Artist 55 chromolithogs. (103 plates reprinted in FINN, F. Indian sporting birds 2nd ed 1917).

LILFORD, T. L. P. *4th Baron* Coloured figures of the birds of the British Islands 1885–1898 7 vols. 421 plates Artist 1 chromolithog. (vol. V. page 58, plate 24 Woodcock).

Caption for Plate facing page 97

Foster's Grey-bellied Tragopan (*Ceriornis blythii* from Hume & Marshall's Game Birds of India 1879 vol. 1. Pl. opposite p. 151) was chromolithographed. The rather stiff portrait was drawn by Foster from a dead specimen.

CLAUDE WILMOTT WYATT

1842-1900

EXCEPT in ornithological circles, this very good artist and author is unknown. He was responsible for some 170 fine hand-coloured plates in two bird books. He was an amateur among the world of professional draughtsmen with big names and reputations at the close of the 19th century.

Wyatt was born on the 2nd March 1842 at Worthing in Sussex. He was the only son of the Vicar of Wroxton and Balscott, the Reverend Thomas Wyatt. He met with a severe accident whilst at Eton, which precluded him from entering a profession, but he continued his education by entering Brasenose College, Oxford. Being free from the ties of a job, he devoted his time and energies to travelling, collecting and studying birds, and to painting them.

From 1869 to 1882 he was generally abroad, visiting Africa, both north and south America, India and other parts of Asia. He joined the 1869 Sinai Expedition as their ornithologist, travelling at his own expense and four years later prepared the report on *Birds of the Ordnance Survey of Sinai*.

Having collected and set up a great number of specimens, he filled his house at Adderbury with glass cases of birds and from 1882 until his death in 1900 he remained quietly at home drawing and painting many bird species.

In association with Dr. Richard Bowdler Sharpe he published two quarto volumes in 1885–94 entitled *A Monograph of the Hirundinidae or Family of Swallows*. All the drawings for each of the 103 plates were done by Wyatt. The work was issued in 20 parts, in which the authors figured and described all the known species of swallows. Dr. Sharpe wrote the text which formed at that time the most up to date and detailed monograph of this family. Wyatt depicted one bird, occasionally a pair, on each plate, ignoring nests, eggs and

C. W. Wyatt

GREEN WOODPECKER

Gecinus viridis

the young of the species. His method of delineating the birds was not detailed. He chose instead to give an outline or impression of the figure. The feathering is not carefully shown, no breast feathers being traced out but represented by "ticks". In his backgrounds, he included much less detail than either J. G. Keulemans or Frohawk would think necessary, only occasionally including a scene or sometimes a number of birds flying. Though the plates are adequate for identification purposes and have a certain amount of charm, they are not as effective or as good as those of these other two artists. Mintern Brothers printed the lithographs but it is not known who coloured them by hand.

Having finished the work on Sharpe's monograph in 1894, Wyatt commenced publishing a work entirely his own. He wrote the text, very short notes on each species, and did the drawings for his *British birds*. In the first volume Wyatt included 25 plates representing 50 species of resident birds. The notes printed on the page opposite each plate were relative to variations in the plumage, all of which could not, of course, be shown in the figures. A companion volume was issued in 1899, having the same short title. The 42 plates of this volume represented 53 British passerine birds. Between them, the two volumes thus depicted over 100 species of birds from the families of the woodpeckers, birds of prey, and pigeons as well as passerines. Mintern Brothers executed the lithographs which were hand-coloured by the Misses Sharpe, to whom Wyatt gives due praise "for the perfect way in which they have carried out the painting for me". Wyatt was fortunate in his colourers, the daughters of Dr. R. B. Sharpe, for they did not over-colour the birds but reproduced their hues faithfully.

The plates vary in the number of species and individuals represented. Sometimes more than one species is included, occasionally both male and female birds of the same species, and, more rarely, a juvenile bird is depicted. Wyatt worked from his large collection of bird skins, though he had seen these species in the field and observed their behaviour. His bird portraits are a little sedate, though life-like for the most part. The bird figures are superimposed on backgrounds of rustic scenes or are shown standing on trees and branches. The colour pattern of the birds in flight is shown by a number of flying birds in the backgrounds of some plates.

Wyatt died on May-day 1900. The very valuable collection of skins which he left was presented by his sister to the Oxford University Museum. Besides the two books mentioned here, Wyatt also had contributed a number of papers on foreign birds to the journal *Ibis*.

CLAUDE WILMOTT WYATT

List of books illustrated by Wyatt

SHARPE, R. B. & WYATT, C. W. A Monograph of the Hirundinidae, or family of swallows 1885–94 2 vols. 103 plates Artist hand-col. lithogs.

WYATT, C. W. British birds, being illustrations of all the species of passerine birds, resident in the British Isles; also picarian birds, birds of prey and pigeons 1894–9 2 vols. 67 plates Artist hand-col. lithogs.

Caption for Plate facing page 100

Wyatt's Green Woodpecker (*Gecinus viridis* from his British Birds vol. II 1899 Pl. opposite p. 21). Wyatt drew this bird from a specimen in his collection. It was lithographed by Mintern Bros. and then hand-coloured.

FREDERICK WILLIAM FROHAWK

1861-1946

Frohawk became a Member of the British Ornithologists' Union in 1895 and a Fellow of the Entomological Society in 1891. Birds and insects were his two main interests in life and his drawings and paintings were largely devoted to these two subjects.

He was born at Brisley Hall, Norfolk on the 16th July 1861, the youngest son of Francis William Frohawk. He was educated in private schools, and then spent his career doing paintings for private commissions, for periodicals and books. His talents were diverse. He worked in oils, water-colours, lithography and wood-engraving. Frohawk was a zoological artist to the *Field* from 1881 onwards being only twenty when he was appointed. He contributed illustrations of birds and reptiles for the *Encyclopaedia Britannica* and fishes for the British Museum *Catalogue of Fishes*, with various subjects for the journal of the *Proceedings* of the Zoological Society, and other associations. To mark his achievements, he was awarded the Civil List Pension of £200 in recognition of services to natural history, and especially entomology. The Entomological Society had previously honoured him in 1926, the year in which his *Natural History of British Butterflies* had been published, by electing him Special Life Fellow.

Apart from this, Frohawk had over one thousand of his drawings reproduced in books about birds. Some were lithographed, some auto-lithographed and others printed by chromolithography.

Frohawk's first bird illustrations appeared in Edward Bartlett's *A Monograph of the weaver-birds and arboreal and terrestrial finches* 1888–9. The single volume had thirty-one plates and was published in five parts, this being all that was issued of a work intended to deal with all known *Ploceidae* and *Fringillidae*. Bartlett (c1836–1908) had been on the Amazon in 1865–9, accompanied H. B. Tristram to Palestine and Syria collecting birds, was a Curator of the Maidstone Museum 1875–90, and then four years after commencing this book he departed for Sarawak and stayed at the Museum in the post of Curator from 1892–6. Despite his wide experience, he was perhaps over ambitious in embarking on so wide a field for he intended to be very thorough in his treatment of each species. The text gives a long synonymy, a detailed description, and collects all available information on habits, habitats, breeding range, etc., for each species. Frohawk's plates are charming. His birds, sometimes single specimens, sometimes the pair of the species, are all drawn standing still, on a branch with a little foliage. Frohawk was both artist and lithographer for the thirty-one plates printed. Had all of the planned ninety-five parts been issued it would have been a monumental work.

Frohawk's next commission for bird-illustrations came from Dr Arthur Gardiner Butler, Assistant Keeper of the Zoology Department of the British Museum from 1897. Dr Butler was also a well-known figure in both entomological and ornithological circles. He had entered the service of the British Museum in 1863 and remained in the insect room for the rest of his working life, retiring in 1901. He was obliged to satisfy his interest in birds in his spare time and was so devoted to the many small birds he kept in his house at Beckenham, that it was believed that he never slept away from home for thirty years.

Dr Butler was writing a book called *Foreign finches in captivity*, with notes on eighty foreign species including their distribution, song and behaviour in captivity. Not all the eighty birds were true members of the finch family. He asked Frohawk to do the illustrations for the sixty hand-coloured plates. A pair of birds of each species is shown on the majority of the plates, with their plumage beautifully and carefully delineated and hand-painted. Their size-scale is given at the foot of each royal octavo plate. Frohawk has given the birds natural background settings, against which the figures stand out clearly and sharply. He was adept at getting his portraits to look fresh, clean-limbed, and to show up clearly against their backgrounds. *Foreign finches in captivity* was issued in 1894–6. A second edition, which is more accurately described as a reprint, had the plates produced by chromolithography. This 1899 reissue is easier to obtain nowadays than the much rarer first edition with hand-coloured illustrations.

Dr Butler had obviously been well-pleased with the drawings of foreign finches for he entrusted the illustrations for his much longer work *British*

FREDERICK WILLIAM FROHAWK

Birds with their nests and eggs to Frohawk. Nearly all of his drawings of the birds on the three hundred and eighteen plates, reproduced in monochrome, are from skins, though Frohawk supplemented many of them with sketches from life. Only three drawings were executed from mounted specimens. Chromolithography was used for the plates depicting eggs. The six volumes were published in the short space of two years, 1896–8. A reprint of the first two volumes with additional colour plates was issued in 1907–08. H. Grönvold contributed some of the new plates. Butler had decided that the text should appeal to both the scientist and layman. He organised the work so that several authors could deal with different classes of birds, writing the first two volumes dealing with *Passeres* himself. These were the volumes reprinted in 1907–08. Frohawk's drawings of eggs were reproduced in colour, those of the birds in monochrome. The birds plates lose much from being uncoloured. Frohawk lightly sketched in the foreground but some of the tree-trunks are more elaborate. Great care was taken with the feathers of the back, wings and tail, but the underparts received scant attention.

An excellent avifauna was compiled by two Cambridge scholars, S. B. Wilson and A. H. Evans in 1890–99. The valuable *Aves Hawaiiensis* about the birds of the Sandwich Islands is a very thorough work based mainly on material collected during a couple of voyages to the islands. The sixty-four coloured plates collected together at the end of the volume were drawn and lithographed by Frohawk. The text is comprehensive and the illustrations are very fine examples of Frohawk's careful work. So often, in lithographic work the general effect is one of diffuse colour and lack of definition. Frohawk manages to have crisper, clear-cut profiles of his birds, and there is little woolliness about his bird pictures.

Interest in the avifauna of the Pacific islands was also shown by Lord Rothschild (1886–1957). He assembled the Tring collections and gathered a great number of bird specimens from foreign countries, at the end of the last century. Lord Rothschild contributed a great deal to the knowledge of the avifauna of Polynesia, the Malay Archipelago and Australia by having collectors in the field and publishing the results of their findings in his journal *Novitates Zoologicae*. Some of the original water-colours for Lord Rothschild's book *Avifauna of Laysan* are still to be seen at Tring, and they compare very favourably with the coloured plates collected together in volume II of *Avifauna of Laysan* published in 1900. Keulemans did most of the eighty-three lithographs but Frohawk contributed a few plates. He autolithographed three plates at the end of volume II, and the nest and eggs of *Chasiempis gayi* (named after Francis Gay who went with the Rothschild expedition 1891) and *Himatione virens*, and two of head and beak details. The book also includes some illustrations of eggs, and some scenes done by Frohawk. There is a picture of albatross nests on Laysan Island and another of guano diggers among the albatrosses. Two further scenes show a wrecked sailor's house, and a lighthouse. Of greater interest is Frohawk's plate of *Porzanula palmeri*, a new bird for which Frohawk had already given the scientific description and name in the *Annals and Magazine of Natural History* (6, 9, 1892). This bird had come from Laysan Island and was named after its collector Henry C. Palmer who was in Lord Rothschild's employ collecting for Tring Museum. The work described the species of birds on Laysan and neighbouring islands and the complete list of these birds comprised one hundred and sixteen forms at that date. Palmer's journey, made December 1890—August 1893 with the purpose of collecting birds, produced one thousand eight hundred and thirty-two specimens, and it was from these that the *Avifauna of Laysan* was compiled.

One different and unlooked-for assignment was given Frohawk at the beginning of the new century. A Russian ornithologist, Sergius Nikola-jewitsch Alpheraky, who was very knowledgeable about geese, wrote a description of most of the old world species. Frohawk was asked to do the illustrations for twenty four chromolithographs. The colour printing of the plates was done by J. N. Kusnerev of Moscow, and they are very beautiful. The text was translated by John Marshall for an English edition published in 1905. Frohawk must have derived great satisfaction from these paintings. The composition is good and the subjects were familiar to him. They depict estuary scenes with a small flock of geese in the distance, and a more detailed close view of one bird in the foreground. They are evocative of the atmosphere of the wide open marshes in the peace of early morning. The colouring of the foregrounds and backgrounds is very subtle. The geese figures are lightly outlined in black so that they stand out clearly. The plates are labelled with indications of the birds' sex, the size reduction, and have Frohawk's mono-gram and the date on which he did the original painting. The red-breasted goose on plate 15 is rather orange-red, but its feathering is quite detailed and crisp. The brent goose on plate 16 is particularly attractive with beautiful soft greys and blue-greys.

The last item to which Frohawk contributed drawings was G. M. Mathew's *Birds of Norfolk and Lord Howe Islands* 1928 and the supplement of 1936. Frohawk worked on twenty-four plates, with Grönvold doing twice that num-ber. Some of the plates showed details of the head and neck, legs and feet of birds, e.g. Frohawk's plate of the brush turkey. In the two volumes issued in

FREDERICK WILLIAM FROHAWK

1928 there were scenes with one bird superimposed, but the supplement plates had few backgrounds. For the supplement Frohawk did a brown-backed little shearwater (*Puffinus lherminieri*) and white-chinned petrel and a garganey duck.

Eighty of Frohawk's original water-colour drawings of birds are preserved in the Natural History Museum. They include a framed painting of a dodo dated 1905 which hangs on the wall outside the library at Tring.

Frohawk's style is very distinctive. Though a careful artist, he also attempted to record an impression of a live bird and something of its character. His paintings are most attractive and deserve much more attention than they have hitherto received.

Books illustrated by Frohawk

ALPHERAKY, S. N. The Geese of Europe and Asia; being the description of most of the old world species (trans. by John Marshall). 1905 25 plates Artist 24 chromolithogs.

BARTLETT, E. A Monograph of the weaver birds (Ploceidae) and arboreal and terrestrial finches (Fringillidae) 1888–9 31 plates hand-col. autolithogs.

BUTLER, A. G. Foreign finches in captivity 1894–6 60 plates hand-col. autolithogs (2nd ed 1899 60 chromolithogs).

BUTLER, A. G. British birds with their nests and eggs 1896–8 6 vols. Artist 318 plates monochrome lithogs + 24 chromolithogs of eggs.

MATHEWS, G. M. Birds of Norfolk and Lord Howe Islands and the Australasian South Polar Quadrant 1928 + Supp. 1936 78 plates Artist 24 hand-col. lithogs.

ROTHSCHILD, L. W. *2nd Baron* The Avifauna of Laysan and the neighbouring islands 1893–1900 83 plates (52 col.) Artist 9 hand-col. lithogs.

TEGETMEIER, W. B. Pheasants for coverts and aviaries: their natural history and practical management 1873 3rd ed 1897 Artist 6 chromolithogs.

WILSON, S. B. & EVANS, A. H. Aves Hawaiiensis: the birds of the Sandwich Islands 1890–99 71 plates (64 col.) 64 hand-col. autolithogs.

Caption for Plate facing page 112

Frohawk's Chatham Island Pigeon (*Hemiphaga chathamensis* from Mathew's A Supplement to the Birds of Norfolk and Lord Howe Islands, 1936 Pl. 77). A plate from the last bird-book to be illustrated with hand-coloured lithographs published in Britain.

HENRIK GRÖNVOLD

1858-1940

GRÖNVOLD was the last of the Continental bird-artists to come to England. Unlike the others, he had no intention of settling in England or of making bird-painting his career. By a series of coincidences he came to be recognised as the successor to Keulemans, and partly filled the Dutchman's place in ornithological illustration when Keulemans became ill.

Henrik Grönvold was born at Praestö in Denmark on 6th September 1858. He had an early love of nature and from his youth he studied and drew the animals and birds in his homeland. He studied drawing in Copenhagen in 1880 and then took a job as an engineering draughtsman. He worked for the Danish artillery, a mill-builder, and then found a more congenial post when he moved to the Danish Biological Research Station in Copenhagen. There he made zoological sketches. He was under the direction of Dr J. G. Petersen for whom he painted and drew fishes.

Finding little opportunity for furthering his career in Denmark, Grönvold decided he would go to America. He came to England, en route for the U.S.A., bearing a letter of introduction to natural history museum authorities. Hearing that the British Museum (Natural History) required an articulator, Grönvold applied for the post and was appointed. He spent some two years preparing bird-skeletons, and then in February 1895 he resigned. He did not leave the museum, but stayed on in an unofficial capacity, working as an artist.

1895 was an important year for Grönvold. Not only did he launch himself, at the age of thirty-seven, as a full-time artist, but he also had an interesting collecting trip to the Salvage Islands with his friend W. R. Ogilvie-Grant. On his return, he married and settled down in this country. He left England on only one other occasion, when he attended an Ornithological Congress in Berlin in 1910.

HENRIK GRÖNVOLD

William Ogilvie-Grant (1863–1924) had been a member of the Natural History Museum staff since 1882 and was to become its Assistant Keeper for the last five years of his service ending in 1918. He organised a number of collecting expeditions to different parts of the world, though he did not accompany each expedition. His friendship with Grönvold resulted in the artist illustrating Ogilvie-Grant's account of the birds brought back from the Mountains of the Moon in Equatorial Africa by the Ruwenzori Expedition of 1905–06. The three hundred and eighty-five species of birds collected were dealt with at the Museum and Ogilvie-Grant gave details of the twenty-seven new species in the *Transactions* of the Zoological Society (volume XIX). Grönvold made the account more valuable by providing figures of the new species and very rare species and also of the eggs of twenty-four species. These drawings were chromolithographed. Ogilvie-Grant fully appreciated Grönvold's remarkable ability to reproduce the matt finish and the texture of birds' eggs. Some of Grönvold's finest plates are of the eggs of different bird species, an aspect of ornithological illustration largely ignored by other artists. Ogilvie-Grant had worked on the final volumes of the *Catalogue of Birds in the British Museum* and then went on to complete the corresponding work on the collection of birds' eggs in the Museum. These took up five volumes and were published between 1901 and 1912. Grönvold's superb drawings of the eggs were chromolithographed on 79 plates.

Professor Alfred Newton had nothing but praise for Grönvold's egg figures and asked him to execute the eight plates of Great Auk eggs for *Ootheca Wolleyana* which he was editing. These plates appeared in the 1907 volume.

Grönvold's first bird painting to be reproduced appears to have been of Pallas's sand-grouse. This was done whilst he was still in Denmark. He contributed one plate with four figures to Kjaebölling's bird book *Scandinaviens Fugle*. This plate had been lithographed by C. Cordts and hand-coloured. His earliest writing on natural history subjects appeared in another Danish publication, *Birds of Naestved*, and were essays of his observations on bird life, published in 1893.

By 1894 Grönvold's qualities as a bird-painter had become known in this country and he began his work for zoological periodicals. Many of the issues of both the *Proceedings* and *Transactions* of the Zoological Society of London had first hand-coloured plates and later chromolithographs after his drawings. The *Ibis* editors employed him from 1899 onwards and he also sent Lord Rothschild some drawings for *Novitates Zoologicae* between the years 1903 and 1936. The *Avicultural Magazine* also printed some plates after his drawings.

HENRIK GRÖNVOLD

Grönvold's first really large task was to do the drawings for Captain George E. Shelley's *Birds of Africa*. Capt. Shelley had retired from military service in order to devote himself to the study of natural history. In his standard work on the birds of the Ethiopian Region (roughly Africa south of the Sahara) he listed 2534 forms of birds in the four volumes issued between 1896 and 1912, among them several new species. As usual, these new birds were the ones to create most interest and to be chosen for the illustrations. The plates showed several new species and genera. Each of Grönvold's plates has most carefully executed bird portraits, usually of the pair of each species, with every detail shown. There are very few plates which have background scenes. As examples of ornithological draughtsmanship, with Grönvold working from skins, the illustrations are excellent. The fifty-seven plates have both figures and plants painstakingly coloured by hand.

After this, commissions came in quick succession for drawings of birds collected in many other countries, including India, South America and Australia. Grönvold worked, in the main, on the large continental avifaunas, and only contributed a small number of plates to two monographs of bird families—Beebe's *Pheasants* and Godman's *Petrels*. The four volumes on the pheasants contained illustrations from photographs and from original paintings, the latter reproduced by either chromolithography or collotype. This work was an interesting example of the period when the older methods of reproduction were being used side by side with the newer photographic methods. Only a few plates from Grönvold's oil paintings were chromo-lithographed, e.g. in vol I Plate VIII where he distinguished clearly the various Tragopon plumages and Plate IV the different colours in the plumage of the Himalayan Blood Pheasants. Seven other artists produced original paintings in oils for this book by Beebe. Thorburn was one of them, and his paintings were largely reproduced by collotype, and G. E. Lodge also produced a few for the ninety coloured plates. The volumes were printed just after the war, 1918–22, and published under the auspices of the New York Zoological Society by Witherby's of London. Not only was this one of the last books to contain chromolithographs, but it was one of the few to be issued in folio format after the war.

One of Grönvold's other early commissions was to draw some Tunisian birds from the collection of about three hundred and fifty species and forms brought home by Joseph I. S. Whitaker, a careful ornithologist and close observer of birds' habits. For the limited edition of only 250 copies Grönvold drew the figures for the nineteen hand-coloured plates in *The Birds of Tunisia*. Several of the plates were accurately coloured by Miss Dora Bowdler Sharpe, one of Dr Sharpe's daughters. The immaculately painted, detailed bird figures are superimposed on elaborate background scenes. Grönvold has succeeded admirably with the larks, *Galerida cristata arenicola* and *G. thekla major*, and also with Tristram's warbler *Melizophilus deserticus*. He was adept at rendering the subtle soft browns and greys of larks and other birds with muted colouring.

Lord Brabourne had been less fortunate with his plans for an account of a country's avifauna, this time of South America. Just before the first world war he was out in South America and a large collection of birds was made. Lord Brabourne (Third Baron, 1885–1915) had enlisted Charles Chubb, an officer at the British Museum, to help him with the descriptions of all the species and genera—enough material to fill sixteen volumes. This was to be illustrated with four hundred hand-coloured plates from drawings by Grönvold. A first volume appeared in 1912 listing the *Birds of South America* but before the next parts were published the war intervened, and then Lord Brabourne died in March 1915. A fine set of plates had already been finished by Grönvold and partially printed, so rather than waste them, they were issued separately. *The Birds of South America vol II (Plates)* had some notes about the birds added by H. K. Swann. It is considered by many critics that the thirty-eight hand-coloured plates were some of the best ever done by Grönvold, so the decision to issue them was fortunate. The plates are of game birds and waterfowl, intended to illustrate volumes II and III. One very attractive plate (Plate 27) illustrates two of the four species of those small relatives of waders, the Seedsnipes, a pair of *Thinocorus orbignyianus* and a pair of *T. rumicivorus* i.e. D'Orbigny's and the Pigmy or Patagonian Seedsnipes.

Another would-be author of a South American avifauna died before completing his work and Charles Chubb was concerned with this publication, along with Grönvold. Chubb (1868–1914) used the notes of F. V. McConnell to describe the *Birds of British Guiana* in 2 volumes 1916–21. The first of the volumes contained twenty chromolithographs after Grönvold's drawings and then the second volume, issued after the war, had illustrations by the 3-colour printing process. Grönvold worked from the large collection of skins obtained by McConnell during two lengthy expeditions into the interior of the country. Grönvold's bird portraits in both these South American avifaunas are detailed, clear delineations of the birds against very little background material. The British Guiana birds were those species whose breeding season and range fell within the territory.

Grönvold needed both skill and imagination for Baker's Indian bird illustrations. Edward Charles Stuart Baker served for many years in the Indian police force. He was also an industrious author and issued a series of volumes dealing with the birds of India, from 1908 over the next twenty-two years. For this series Grönvold drew many ducks, pigeons and game birds. His most elaborate backgrounds are seen in these lithographs. Often they are too dark and cluttered. The *Game Birds* illustrations were printed on yellow tinted paper and the effect of the dark backgrounds and coloured paper is not pleasing. Grönvold's bird-figures, when seen against those of Lodge, in the three titles are less detailed, but his settings and scenes are more vigorous than those of Keulemans, another of Baker's illustrators, who tends to be still painting pretty pictures in the style of Gould. Baker's own designs are different again. He gives broad general impressions of the birds which are placed on a branch, with the only additional decoration being an occasional flowering plant or nest. Baker's plates are much simpler in design than those of the "museum artists". Many of Grönvold's drawings for Baker's *Indian pigeons and doves*, for Shelley and for Howard (mentioned later) are now in the McGill University Library, Montreal.

After the first world war, very few books were produced with chromolithographic illustrations and hardly any with hand-coloured lithographs. Grönvold worked on the very last of the hand-coloured lithographs used to illustrate a bird-book by Australian-born Gregory Macalister Mathews (1876–1949). Mathews made a fortune in mining early in life. On marrying a lady who had two children by her first husband the family moved to England in 1902 in order to educate the children in this country. Mathews bought a house, Langley Mount, mid-way between Tring Zoological Museum and the Natural History Museum in London and devoted himself to ornithology. He discovered that very little had been written in the last few years about Australian birds and that there was not a great deal of material available in the museums here for studying the Australian avifauna. He collected books and specimens of Australian birds and employed collectors to work for him in Australia. So, by degrees, he came to embark on a very ambitious undertaking, a comprehensive treatise on Australian birds. Much more information had come to light during the seventy years since Gould's fine avifauna *The Birds of Australia* had been published in 1840–8. With thirty thousand specimens now in his collection, Mathews set to work to describe each genera and species and employed a number of artists to do the work for the six hundred hand-coloured lithographs for the twelve volumes published between 1910 and 1927. Grönvold was the obvious choice for the work, and Mathews and he must often have consulted one another at the Natural History Museum in South Kensington. He was responsible for three hundred and sixty of the

. Frohawk

CHATHAM ISLAND PIGEON

Hemiphaga chathamensis

H. Grönvold

1. RED-TAILED GUAN   2. RED-WINGED GUAN
Ortalida ruficauda   Ortalida erythroptera

plates for *Birds of Australia*, thus contributing well over half the drawings, some of which appeared in every one of the twelve volumes. His careful work on the bird figures, boughs and leaves is seen at its best in this large quarto treatise. Particularly noticeable is his facility in accurate portrayal of the small rather nondescript birds or "little brown jobs" with their subtle colouring. The plates have no scenes or backgrounds, the bird figures being placed on rocks by the sea and on shore, or on branches, as appropriate. The figures include about one hundred species discovered since the days of Gould.

Not content with completing this mammoth task, Mathews started work on a complementary text for the *Birds of Norfolk and Lord Howe Islands* (1928) and then a supplement which covered the birds not included in Buller's *Birds of New Zealand*. By 1936 the Australasian avifauna was comprehensively recorded and depicted. Mathews had supplied the deficiencies he had found on coming to England some thirty years before. The 1936 supplement was the last bird-book to have hand-coloured lithographs and was printed by Witherby. Grönvold's treatment is slightly different in the forty-eight plates he did for this work. His beautifully clear impressions of the birds, usually the pair of the species, are set on a branch with leaves and a "wash" colour background, but some plates have more elaborate backgrounds. Once again, it is the small birds which are best. The criticism that Grönvold's birds are stiff portraits can be levelled. Grönvold uses so few different attitudes and stances for his birds that when leafing through a book illustrated by him the pictures all seem to show the birds in the same, or very similar, positions. Apart from very small bird figures in some of his backgrounds, none are shown in flight, and the ducks when placed on water are more like decoy ducks than living creatures.

Of all the lithographs and chromolithographs worked from Grönvold's drawings, most probably the best known and liked were those done quite early in his career for H. E. Howard's *The British Warblers*. When Henry Eliot Howard was writing his remarkable book about British warblers he was concerned not only with their descriptions and notes of habitat, etc., as other authors before him, but he tried to understand their behaviour and to interpret their world. He also expounded his theory of sexual selection and revealed that birds behave territorially. To illustrate this classic, both chromolithographs and photogravure plates were used. Thirty-five of the chromolithographs were printed by W. Greve of Berlin after drawings by Grönvold. Here Grönvold is relaxed, dealing with birds he had seen alive and in their natural habitats. He used simple background "washes" or muted colours and placed a pair of birds in the foreground. The bird-figures have very soft plumage and feathering which is delicately drawn, but in strange contrast, the birds are a little stiff and lacking in life. The plates are collected together at the end of the volumes, the first having seventeen chromolithographs and the second eighteen. Ten of the pencil drawings Grönvold made for *British Warblers* are kept in the Natural History Museum in London. There are a number of his water-colour drawings of birds also in this collection.

As a result of Grönvold's early training and work as a draughtsman and then as an articulator he had a special insight into the problems confronting anatomical draughtsmen. His own anatomical drawings reached a very high standard and he drew anatomical plates for Dr P. R. Lowe of the Bird Room. He also drew fishes and reptiles for the Museum staff.

Grönvold's work became known to many more members of the public when he drew a number of designs for the postcards issued by the British Museum. The water-colour drawings of birds and their eggs, done for this series of postcards, are preserved at the Natural History Museum.

He continued to draw and paint to an advanced age, his later work being reproduced by photographic processes. He had his share of illness, sustaining a nasty fall just after the war in which he broke a leg and was obliged to use a stick thereafter whilst walking. His sight was impaired by a cataract on one eye and he thought his painting days were over. After much persuasion by his friends, he was eventually induced to have the cataract removed and was then delighted to find he could draw as well as ever.

He died peacefully in Bedford Hospital in March 1940, his wife having died five years previously, leaving a daughter Elsa, who was also an artist. Grönvold was a modest, quiet man, who was generous in his admiration of the work of other artists whilst being diffident about his own considerable achievements.

Books illustrated by Henrik Grönvold

BAKER, E. C. S. Indian ducks and their allies 1908 30 plates Artist 17 hand-col. lithogs.

BAKER, E. C. S. Game birds of India, Burma and Ceylon 1921–30 3 vols. 60 plates (30 lithogs from Indian ducks, and 30 additional plates) Artist 19 hand-col. lithogs in vol. I; 19 hand-col. lithogs in vol. II; (all 11 photographic plates in vol. III).

BEEBE, C. W. A Monograph of the pheasants 1918–22 4 vols. 90 col. plates Artist for 13 plates—a few chromolithogs.

BRABOURNE, W. W. K.—H. *3rd Baron* & CHUBB, C. The birds of South America 1913 vol. II Plates; edited by H. K. Swann 1917 38 plates Artist 38 hand-col. lithogs.

BRITISH MUSEUM (Natural History) Catalogue of the collection of birds' eggs 1901–1912 5 vols. 79 plates Artist 79 chromolithogs.

BUTLER, A. G. Birds of Great Britain and Ireland: Order Passeres 1904–08 2 vols. 115 plates (8 chromolithogs of eggs + 107 of birds) (A reprint of first two vols. of British Birds with their nests and eggs 6 vols. 1896–8) A few additional plates by Grönvold.

CHUBB, C The birds of British Guiana, based on the collection of Fred. Vavasour McConnell 1916–21 2 vols. Artist 20 chromolithogs.

GODMAN, F. du Cane A monograph of the petrels 1907–10 2 vols. 106 plates Artist 3 hand-col. lithogs.

HOWARD, H. E. The British warblers: a history with problems of their lives 1907–14 2 vols. 98 plates Artist 35 chromolithogs.

Ibis volumes from 1899–1940.

KJAERBÖLLING, N. Scandinaviens Fugle (Ny Tavle III til...) Plate X, 1 with four figures—hand-col. lithog. (1893?).

MATHEWS, G. M. The birds of Australia 1910–27 12 vols. (+ 5 supps.) 600 plates Artist 360 hand-col. lithogs.

MATHEWS, G. M. The birds of Norfolk and Lord Howe Islands and the Australasian South Polar Quadrant 1928 45 plates A Supplement to the Birds of Norfolk and Lord Howe Islands, to which is added those birds of New Zealand not figured by Buller. 1936 57 plates Artist 48 hand-col. lithogs in the two vols.

Novitates Zoologicae: a journal of zoology in connection with the Tring Museum—volumes from 1903 to 1936.

SHELLEY, G. E. & SCLATER, W. L. The birds of Africa, comprising all the species which occur in the Ethiopian Region 1896–1912 5 vols. 81 plates Artist 57 hand-col. lithogs.

WHITAKER, J. I. S. The birds of Tunisia: being a history of the birds in the Regency of Tunis 1905 2 vols. 19 plates Artist 19 hand-col. lithogs.

WOLLEY, J. Ootheca Wolleyana: an illustrated catalogue of the collection of birds' eggs, begun by the late John Wolley jun. and continued with additions by Alfred Newton 1864–1907 2 vols. 38 plates Artist 8 chromolithogs in vol. 2 (Plates XIV-XXI N-P).

ZOOLOGICAL SOCIETY OF LONDON Proceedings, Transactions.

Caption for Plate facing page 113

Grönvold's Red-tailed and Red-winged Guans (*Ortalida ruficauda* and *O. erythroptera* from Brabourne & Chubb's Birds of South America vol. ii 1917 Pl. 9) from a series containing Grönvold's best work for the lithographic medium.

ARCHIBALD THORBURN

1860-1935

THORBURN AND LODGE were both born in 1860, though Lodge was to outlive Thorburn by some eighteen years. Despite Lodge's longevity, his work was overshadowed by that of Thorburn. Lodge's birds of prey might well have excelled Thorburn's paintings of those particular birds, but in every other sphere few artists could rival Thorburn.

He had a most advantageous start to life as an artist since he was the son of the famous miniaturist Robert Thorburn (1818–1885). On the 31st May 1860, when Archibald was born, his parents were living at Lasswade in Midlothian, near Edinburgh. He was educated in Scotland, first in Dalkeith and later Edinburgh. Then his father sent him to attend an art school in St John's Wood, London, but Thorburn later said that he learned more from his father than from any other teacher.

His earliest compositions were flower pictures, and he continued to paint flowers and take an additional interest in them as a keen horticulturalist. He also enjoyed painting landscapes, and was excellent at this form of painting. He had a gift for placing his bird subjects in harmonious surroundings so that the birds and their background were perfectly matched and made a completely satisfying picture. Though these landscapes were beautifully painted, it must be admitted that from a scientific point of view they were, very occasionally, not entirely appropriate to the bird. He was not good at figure painting but recognised his limitations and concentrated on the work he did best. His favourite subjects were birds, so he spent most of his time painting them. His interest in birds was not solely as an artist, but also as a sportsman and field-observer. The combination of all these interests, inclinations and abilities helped him to produce some of the finest bird paintings of all time.

116

ARCHIBALD THORBURN

Thorburn painted almost entirely in water-colours, supplemented with flake-white for various special effects. His subjects were not so successfully portrayed in oils, and he did few paintings in that medium. His original paintings were popular and sold well in London. In the last decade of the century he exhibited a number of pictures at the Royal Academy, though he was disappointed in the selectors' choice on one occasion when he had the sympathy of Lord Lilford who tried to console him with the comment, "I am very sorry to hear that your pictures have been crowded out at the R.A. and wish I could think that equally good ones had been crowded in." (Letter, 20 April 1891).

The first time his work was reproduced for a bird-book was when James Edmund Harting's *Sketches of Bird-life* was published in 1883. Thorburn's contribution consisted of two figures (pages 10 and 92) in black and white, one of a kestrel and the other of a group of blue titmice. Three titles with chromolithographs after his drawings concern us here. These drawings were commissioned by Lord Lilford, Walter Swaysland and L. H. L. Irby.

Walter Swaysland, a Brighton naturalist and taxidermist, was nearly at the end of his life when he employed the twenty-three year old Thorburn to help illustrate *Familiar wild birds*, published in parts between 1883 and 1888. Swaysland just completed this work before he died. He had collected many rare birds on the Sussex coast for ornithologists of that period, but it was the familiar birds of the countryside about which he chose to write. Each of the four volumes had thirty-six coloured plates of birds and four coloured plates of their eggs. Over one hundred of the bird plates are the first coloured reproductions of Thorburn's water-colour drawings, but all of the pictures in this small book are charming. They had a single bird on each plate with suitable plants in the foreground. Thorburn has been careful to delineate each feather in its place and has also managed to convey a feeling of the texture of the very soft plumage of many of the birds. The plates were chromolithographed for the first edition, in a later edition they were reprinted using the three-colour process. This book demonstrated Thorburn's facility in painting the small birds with a degree of charm and daintiness of which Wolf and Lodge were not capable, and only Keulemans came anywhere near achieving.

Before the final volume of *Familiar wild birds* had been issued, Lord Lilford's chief artist, Keulemans, had been taken ill and Lord Lilford approached Thorburn with a view to his making some drawings for him. Thorburn began work for Lord Lilford in 1887 and completed the drawings for his share of *Coloured figures*, two hundred and sixty-eight of them, ten years later—an average of one per fortnight. Working for Lord Lilford was exacting, for the Baron kept a very tight control over the work of his artists. In the biography of Lord Lilford by his sister, Mrs C. M. Drewitt, there is a series of letters from Lord Lilford to Thorburn carrying detailed instructions for, and criticisms of, Thorburn's paintings. Lord Lilford is commendatory, always polite, but insistent on absolute accuracy. He was prepared to go to great lengths to obtain specimens and live birds from which Thorburn could take accurate drawings and to inform him where to go for his models. He laid down the composition of the picture, the number of birds, which state of plumage, how many representatives of the species he required and the posture of the individual birds. One example of a letter from Lord Lilford to Thorburn will suffice to show the degree of oversight he exercised and the relationship between them—unmistakably that of patron and paid artist.

"Lilford January 20, 1891

"I am sending you today four skins of Pomatorhine Skua from the coast of Norfolk, and a skin of Ross's Wedge-tailed Gull lent to me by Professor Newton. You will probably be able to borrow a more full adult P. Skua than any of these from Dresser, but there are some good varieties of plumage in these. If you do not think that three figures would crowd a plate too much I should like to have the most fully adult bird that you can procure as the principal foreground figure, the most uni-coloured bird of those sent in the near background, and one of the strongly *barred* birds on the wing. If this is too much for one plate we must have two, with adult and strongly barred young one in the first, and two of most widely divergent types in the other, a flat sea-coast scene.

In Ross's Gull I should be glad if you could make the wedge-shaped tail as conspicuous as possible, and the breast may be brilliantly rose-coloured. An Arctic-sea scene with cloudless pale-blue sky and broken ice-floe, *not bergs*, will best suit this plate."

There was not much room for manoeuvre there, even if Thorburn wished to give the pictures something of his own personality.

Thorburn was not expected to work entirely from skins. Lord Lilford had many live members of bird species in his aviaries and on his pools at Lilford and there were plenty more of the birds he had collected, or their later generations, living in the Zoological Gardens in London. There were cranes in the pinetum at Lilford and birds of prey in the falconer's quarters. If specimens were required, they could be obtained from the Hon. Walter Rothschild collection at Tring or seen at the Natural History Museum in London.

ARCHIBALD THORBURN

Among the birds in Lord Lilford's collection, painted by Thorburn for Lord Lilford's personal enjoyment, were an Egyptian Vulture, sketched in 1890; adult and young night herons, a bittern and a lammergeier, all painted in 1887; a skua brought from Foula 1891; and a Montagu's harrier whose portrait was done in 1893.

Lord Lilford would very much have liked Wolf, whom he admired greatly, to do some drawings for his book, but the elderly bird-artist was no longer undertaking work of this kind. Lord Lilford compromised when he got Thorburn to make four studies of capercaillie, gyrfalcon, an adult female Iceland falcon and a red-footed falcon, after drawings by Wolf. These were all printed and may be seen in volume I of *Coloured figures*. Thorburn's own work on an immature Iceland falcon, a Greenland falcon and a peregrine compare favourably with those birds of prey done after Wolf. Thorburn's eagles, among other raptores which he painted, are also majestic, awe-inspiring portraits.

George Lodge did six plates for Lord Lilford, but one of them gave cause for some complaints from subscribers. The turtle dove (in volume IV Plate 42) was not on the same scale or in the same style as the other plates. The plate was not withdrawn or suppressed by Lord Lilford, but he asked Thorburn to do an additional "turtle dove plate", to be sold separately to subscribers who wished to purchase this extra plate. Only one hundred copies were printed by Greve of Berlin, Lord Lilford's best lithographic printers, and these were snapped up at 12/- each and many more could have been sold. Copies of *Coloured figures* with the additional plate bound in are consequently very rare and today fetch a high price when placed on the market.

Thorburn went to Lilford on a number of occasions. During one visit he did a water-colour drawing of Lilford Hall. Lord Lilford was, by this time, confined to a bath chair with hereditary rheumatic gout, but this did not deter him from taking a keen interest in the progress of the book, compiling the text and writing numerous letters (though the actual writing was often done for him by his wife as his hands were crippled and painful) to his many correspondents. He did not live to see the last three parts of the work published for he died in 1896, when sixty-three years old.

When completed and bound into seven volumes, *Coloured figures* had four hundred and twenty-one chromolithographs. Thorburn was responsible for nearly two-thirds of the plates. Lord Lilford's brief description of every British species known at that time, was accompanied by one or more portraits of each species. The plates are very beautiful, Thorburn's being among the best in the book. His range is quite astonishing for he is excellent with the

119

game birds and wildfowl, did charming portraits of the small birds, and his owls and birds of prey are very convincing. Thorburn did all the gulls, guillemots, plovers and nearly all the ducks, geese, sandpipers, terns and skuas, as well as the crow family. Each part when published had a colourful variety of bird forms to make them more interesting e.g. the first part including Thorburn's birds (no. vii) contained an alpine accentor, linnet, rose-coloured pastor, pied woodpecker, night heron, hoopoe, bittern, sooty shearwater and Bulwer's petrel by him, and three other plates by other artists making up the dozen for this part. When all the parts had been issued, the plates and corresponding text were reassembled and arranged in bird families before being bound into the seven volumes.

There had been a number of books on British birds before this one, but Lord Lilford had wanted to give as many people as possible the opportunity to possess beautiful pictures of our own native birds and had kept the cost as low as he could to the subscribers (though it cost him some £15,000). He had also been anxious to record the different states of plumage and took great care to note on the plates the sex and age of each bird figured, and also the amount of reduction in size of the figure. The male and female birds of large species had a whole plate devoted to each of them. Some chicks were included e.g. Thorburn's Tengmalm's owl, a magnificent plate, has a fluffy chick (vol. I Pl. 143). The smaller birds have only one plate per pair. Thorburn's grouse have moorland scenes in the background, some plates have more elaborate background detail. Lord Lilford dealt honourably with his artists allowing each plate to bear the name or monogram of the artist, lithographer and the printer.

Though it proved an exceedingly inconvenient arrangement, Lord Lilford used a Berlin lithographic printer, W. Greve, for most of the plates. He frequently complained at their slowness in sending completed prints, but since their two hundred and sixty-three plates proved so good in quality of reproduction and colour, he decided that he could not dispense with their services. Among the English lithographers were Hanhart, Mintern Brothers (who produced the highest number of prints after Greve) and West & Newman. Some of the best of the English lithographs were done by the firm Chromo-Litho Art Studios who were responsible for forty-four of the plates.

The whole format of the book is beautiful and expensive-looking. The plates are considered to be some of the best coloured pictures of birds ever produced for a book. Considering the high quality, the thirty-six parts of the first edition, published at 9/6d per part, were very good value. Copies of the

A. Thorburn

EAGLE OWL

Bubo maximus, *Fleming*

second edition parts cost more, being 12/- per part, but the plates were improved upon in many instances and this is the better edition from the point of view of both accuracy and quality of the plates. A copy of the seven volumes of the first edition would cost about £300 today. Though it might not be easy for modern readers to see Thorburn's work in *Coloured figures*, the plates have been reproduced in a number of publications of Messrs Warne, e.g. in T. Coward's *Birds of the British Isles*, but they are not as good as the chromolithographs from which they were taken.

A companion of Lord Lilford's early days when he travelled abroad frequently, was Lt-Col. L. H. L. Irby. He did service at Gibraltar and was able to collect material whilst there for his publication *The Ornithology of the Straits of Gibraltar*. Another companion, Col. W. W. C. Verner did a lot of active field work in the same area, and his notes were incorporated in the second edition of Irby's book issued in 1895. This edition also had eight plates from drawings by Thorburn and some six photographic plates taken from Verner's work. Thorburn's birds were set in scenery of the typical habitat of the species, and included a bearded vulture, which was used for the frontispiece, black and cinerous vultures, golden eagle, white-shouldered eagle, Mediterranean peregrine, and a European bush quail. Irby is said to have issued this small avifauna at the instigation of Lord Lilford who was very interested in the area having cruised there in his own yacht. At this time Irby was considered to be the best authority on the birds of southern Spain and Gibraltar.

Why are Thorburn's birds, nearly all of them shown standing on perches (he frankly admitted his inability to paint birds in flight), so lively and lifelike when many other artists fail to convey any feeling of life even when their birds are "active", that is, depicted flying, preening, etc? It is always difficult to convey in words the atmosphere of a work of art. Nevertheless, there are certain characteristics of Thorburn's painting technique which give us clues to his success. He could paint water successfully, an ability which helped greatly as so many of his paintings were of water-side birds. He could manage the delicate painting required for little birds, no detail being too finicky for him. The beautiful little down feathers of the breast straying over the wing coverts were always shown in delicate tracery and were not cut off by a hard outline contour of the wing. He could reproduce the very soft plumage with great fidelity—his owls being particularly good. Thorburn also painted birds' eyes correctly. So often bird-artists mismanage this tiny but vital part of their portraits and produce replicas of dead-looking or glass eyes. Thorburn accurately places the tiny speck of white which gives "life" not only to the eye, but to the whole personality of the bird. In addition, his birds are always solid, not flat cardboard, figures.

Thorburn's technique may have been faultless but that alone would not have achieved such magnificent bird portraits. His field knowledge adds a dimension which immediately sets him above Neale, Keulemans, etc. who worked almost exclusively from skins. Thorburn was a sportsman and saw his birds as part of their backgrounds. He was a landscape painter and his pictures of birds' environment for the most part suits their characters. His colouring of the background is excellent, just as his birds are accurately coloured, the two blending together as nature intended.

Thorburn knew that to reconcile the sportsman's fleeting view of birds and the scientist's demand for still-life accuracy, was impossible. Yet in a remarkable way he went further along the road to achieving the impossible than anyone else. His birds are scientifically accurate without his artistic settings being incongruous. When shown in a large vista, such as a moorland setting, the bird figures are small, though still accurate, portraits. His close-up views are exact replicas of the live birds. It is unusual to find an artist equally good at painting a large picture with groups of birds and depicting a single specimen with great accuracy on a small scale.

There are a few less successful paintings. His terns in Lord Lilford's work are not as good as his other birds, and perhaps the gulls, too, are not entirely successful. It is not that white birds proved difficult, for his snowy owl is superb and the snow goose excellent. The only recurring criticism of Lord Lilford's concerning a number of Thorburn's drawings was that birds were "too plump". Perhaps the terns are not sufficiently streamlined. This plumpness, of course, gives the birds substance, but may be a little overdone in the pictures of the *Laridae*.

At the end of the 19th century, Thorburn, still a comparatively young man was already reaping the reward for his industry and talent. He was elected a Fellow of the Zoological Society in 1898 and became a Member of the British Ornithologists' Union in 1900. Commissions for his pictures were pouring in from customers who wanted them on their walls, and authors who wanted to reproduce them in their books about birds. Authors on the Continent were among the many seeking his services. His pictures were far more numerous than his illustrations for books, and today when these change hands, they do so at high prices and are much sought after.

A permanent exhibition of both Thorburn's and George Lodge's paintings was opened at the Thorburn-Lodge Gallery at Liskeard, Cornwall, in November 1973. This gallery gives an unrivalled opportunity to see the original work of these two very good bird-artists.

In the 20th century Thorburn produced three books of his own, but unfortunately his drawings for them were reproduced photographically and so do not concern us here. This is a pity, for in his own books, of course, he worked to his own design and the composition of the plates was his own free choice and not painted to order as those for Lord Lilford. Reproductions of many of his own plates can be seen in James Fisher's one-volume edition of *Thorburn's birds* published by Michael Joseph in 1967.

Thorburn was a life-long supporter of the Royal Society for the Protection of Birds and when Baird Carter, the owner of the shop in Jermyn Street where his pictures were sold, suggested he could draw an annual Christmas card for the Society, Thorburn agreed at once. That was in 1899, and Thorburn drew the designs for the 1899, 1905, 1916–1919 and 1923–35 R.S.P.B. cards, giving them as a gift to help the birds which he so much enjoyed watching and painting and which had given him so much pleasure.

He was always willing to share his knowledge and technique with other artists. He sincerely admired George Lodge and was modest when it came to assessing his own work. Despite a long illness during his last years he was cheerful and patient and continued to paint even when ill and lying in bed. He died on 9th October 1935 at Hascombe, Godalming, where he had gone to live after the first world war. He had married Miss Constance Mudie in 1896 and on his death left one son.

Books illustrated by Thorburn

DRESSER, H. E. A History of the birds of Europe, including all the species inhabiting the western Palaearctic region 1871–81 Supplement 1895–6 89 plates 5 hand-col. lithogs copied from originals by Wolf and Thorburn.

IRBY, L. H. L. The Ornithology of the Straits of Gibraltar 1875 2nd ed 1895 14 plates Artist for 8 chromolithographs.

LILFORD, T. L. P. *4th Baron* Coloured figures of the birds of the British Islands 1885–98 7 vols. 421 plates Artist 264 chromolithogs + drawer of 4 designs after J. Wolf also chromolithogs.

SWAYSLAND, W. Familiar wild birds 1883–8 160 plates Artist 105 signed chromolithogs.

Caption for Plate facing page 120

Thorburn's Eagle Owl (*Bubo maximus* from Lilford's Coloured Figures of the Birds of the British Isles 1885 vol. 1. Pl. 46) was chromolithographed and shows the fidelity with which Thorburn depicted beautifully marked feathers.

GEORGE EDWARD LODGE

1860-1953

GEORGE LODGE was an outstanding artist, rivalling Wolf and bettering Thorburn in his ability to paint birds of prey. Born in 1860, the same year as Thorburn, he was to live, hale and hearty, to the ripe old age of 93, painting to the last. Lodge saw the end of the production of the fine folio bird books illustrated with hand-coloured lithographs and chromolithographs and continued working long enough to see hundreds of his drawings translated into book illustrations by photographic means. As a bird-artist he was most appreciated at the end of his long life when some of his best work was reproduced in the twelve volumes of Bannerman's *Birds of the British Isles*. With this work he achieved his life's ambition to draw all our native birds.

Out of a large Lincolnshire family of eight children, two boys were to become famous ornithologists, George and his brother R. B. Lodge. Reginald Lodge was a pioneer of bird photography and was awarded the Royal Photographic Society's first medal for natural history in 1895. The two brothers were keen naturalists from an early age and roamed the Lincolnshire fields and fens in search of birds, their nests and eggs. They were to be seen, in the 1870s, pushing a wheelbarrow containing a 12″ x 10″ plate camera over hill and dale on their field excursions. Reginald's enthusiasm for bird photography earned a sympathetic though not equally committed response from George.

George Lodge's enthusiasm was for painting birds. He had also been collecting and stuffing specimens from the age of twelve. To develop his talents his father sent him to the Lincoln School of Art, where he won fourteen prizes, and then he was apprenticed to a wood engraver and became expert at engraving bird figures. Some of his wood-engravings were used by Howard Saunders in *An illustrated manual of British birds* published in 1889, and another hundred for W. H. Hudson's *British birds* 1895.

G. E. Lodge

PEREGRINE FALCON
AND PTARMIGAN
Falco peregrinus and Lagopus mutus

GEORGE EDWARD LODGE

His skill as a taxidermist enabled Lodge to have a clear understanding of birds' physical make-up and he was fond of saying that it was impossible to draw the outside of a bird satisfactorily without an intimate knowledge of the inside structure. His studio held mounted specimens of birds of prey and, not neglecting the live birds, his garden was a sanctuary for many species. He was a quiet, gentle person, and the birds around his home fearlessly approached him and perched close to him, when he was sitting outside, whilst they accepted crumbs from his fingers. He also owned falcons, becoming a keen falconer, and regularly walked about London with a falcon on his wrist.

His bird-paintings were meticulous, almost photographic, copies of their originals. He painted each bird exactly as he saw it, with its plumage flaws and its own characteristic expression, in natural surroundings. The backgrounds to his pictures received the same close attention and were painted in great detail. For evidence of this see his pheasants which were painted in oils for Beebe.

Lodge received many commissions to paint pictures for private collectors. These included sporting scenes and birds of prey. Thorburn and he were not in competition in this area for Thorburn specialised in painting game birds and Lodge concentrated on the birds of prey, his special favourites being the falcons. Lodge had a wide circle of friends in all walks of life and was a gregarious character. He fished and shot game on many country estates and his original paintings are scattered throughout a large number of country houses in England and Scotland. One of the connoisseurs who bought Lodge's pictures was Lord Rothschild who had 5 of Lodge's water-colour drawings of birds framed. These were acquired for the national collection as part of the Rothschild bequest in 1937. This was the type of work Lodge found most congenial. He disliked the amount of reduction in size which book-work involved. He was born too late for the large folio books in which the birds were lithographed life-size. They belonged to a past era and he was unfortunate not to get commissions for the few remaining titles using this size and format.

Most of Lodge's lithographed plates appeared in Baker's works on Indian birds. There his meticulously detailed birds were set against simple, light-coloured backgrounds, in great contrast with the heavy, dark backgrounds of Grönvold. The bird figures, usually a pair on each plate, are drawn in every detail right down to the scales on the feet.

On 7th July 1887 Lord Lilford wrote in a letter, "I had seen some of Mr Lodge's work before. His drawings are admirable; I must try and make acquaintance with him." In this he succeeded, and the following April was writing to Lodge himself about various birds of prey. Lodge only did one or two plates for Lord Lilford however (one of them a Turtle Dove), despite this hint that more would develop. A drawing which Lodge did for the Baron was of a Goshawk besieged i.e. a Goshawk on a block face to face with a dog. This is reminiscent of Wolf and his delight in depicting a dramatic scene from nature. Lord Lilford's letters show another pleasing facet of Lodge's character, his unstinting praise for Thorburn's work. In a letter to Thorburn, concerning some drawings he had sent for *Coloured figures*, Lord Lilford says (July 31, 1890) "The drawings and plates arrived this morning. I have nothing but unqualified admiration to bestow upon them, and Mr Lodge, who is at least as good a judge of birds as I am, and an infinitely superior critic of art, is entirely of my opinion."

Lodge's type of bird-illustration, the realistic recording of every detail exactly as he saw it, has largely been taken over by the use of the camera. For close-ups in canvas and oils, however, Lodge stands supreme in this century for raptores and the larger birds, though his technique was not equally successful with the smaller birds.

Books with lithographic illustrations after drawings by Lodge

BAKER, E. C. S. The Indian ducks and their allies 1908 30 plates Artist 4 hand-col. lithogs.

BAKER, E. C. S. The game birds of India, Burma and Ceylon 1921–30 75 plates (60 col.) (30 lithogs from Indian ducks + 30 additional plates) Artist 2 hand-col. lithogs in vol. I, both ducks.

BEEBE, C. W. A Monograph of the pheasants 1918–22 4 vols. 90 col. plates Artist for 43 col. plates, some collotype, some chromolithogs.

LILFORD, T. L. P. *4th Baron* Coloured figures of the birds of the British Islands 1885–98 7 vols. 421 plates Artist 6 chromolithogs.

MATHEWS, G. M. Birds of Australia 1910–27 12 vols. 600 plates Artist 1 hand-col. lithog in vol. V—pl. 254.

Caption for Plate facing page 124

Lodge's Peregrine and Ptarmigan (*Falco peregrinus* and *Lagopus mutus* from Col. T. Thornton's A Sporting Tour through the northern parts of England and great part of the Highlands of Scotland, 1896. Originally published 1804) is an early picture of a falcon drawn by Lodge at the end of the 19th century, for Lemercier of Paris to chromolithograph. It is one of four Lodge plates which illustrate the reprint of this book by a famous 18th century sportsman.

BIBLIOGRAPHY

ANKER, J. Bird books and bird art. 1938.

BARRETT, C. L. The bird man: a sketch of the life of John Gould. 1938.

Bird Notes & News 1946, xxii, no. 4, pp. 52–4 Fisher, J. Gould and Wolf.

BLAND, D. A history of book illustration. 1958.

BOASE, F. Modern English biography 6 vols. 1965 reprint.

BOOTH, E. T. Catalogue of the cases of birds in the Dyke Road Museum, Brighton. 1901.

British Birds 1912, 6, p. 58 Obituary of Keulemans by G. M. Mathews. 1935, 29, p. 172 Obituary of Thorburn by G. E. Lodge. 1940, 33, p. 333 Obituary of Grönvold by N. B. Kinnear.

BRYAN, M. A biographical dictionary of painters and engravers; edited by G. C. Williamson 5 vols 1903–5.

BURCH, R. M. Colour printing and colour-printers. 1911.

CHISHOLM, A. H. Strange new world: the adventures of John Gilbert and Ludwig Leichhardt. 1941. (for chap. on Gould)

DAVIDSON, A. Edward Lear, landscape painter and nonsense poet. 1938.

Dictionary of National Biography

DREWITT, C. M. Lord Lilford: a memoir by his sister, 1900.

Emu 1938–9, xxxviii, pp. 90–95 Iredale, T. John Gould the bird man. pp. 95–118 Hindwood, K. A. John Gould in Australia. pp. 118–131 Dickison, D. J. A résumé of Gould's major works. pp. 138–141 Campbell, A. G. John Gould amongst Tasmanian birds. 1939–50, xlix, pp. 208–210 Hindwood, K. A. A note on William Swainson. 1941, xl, pp. 337–354 Chisholm, A. H. Mrs. Gould and her relatives.

Gentleman's Magazine 1856, pp. 532–3 Obituary of W. Swainson.

GLADSTONE, H. S. Handbook to Lilford's coloured figures of the birds of the British Islands. 1917.

HUGHES, T. Prints for the collector. 1970.

Ibis 1881, pp. 288–290 Obit. of J. Gould. 1901, pp. 347–348 Obit. of C. W. Wyatt. 1925, p. 262 Obit. of W. Foster. 1936. pp. 205–207 Obit. of A. Thorburn. 1940, pp. 545–547 Obit. of H. Grönvold. 1954, p. 474 Obit. of G. E. Lodge.

LEAR, E. Letters of Edward Lear to Chichester Fortescue, Lord Carlingsford and

BIBLIOGRAPHY

Frances, Countess Waldegrave; edited by Lady Strachey. 1907.

LEWIS, C. T. C. The story of picture printing in England during the 19th century. 1927.

LODGE, G. E. Memoirs of an artist naturalist. 1946.

MACLEAN, R. Victorian book design and colour printing. 1963.

MULLENS, W. H. & SWANN, H. K. A bibliography of British ornithology from the earliest times to the end of 1912, including bibliographical accounts of the principal writers and bibliographies of their published works. 1917.

Nature 1881, xxiii, pp. 364–5, 491 Obit. of J. Gould.

NISSEN, C. Die illustrierten Vogelbücher: ihre Geschichte und Bibliographie. 1953.

NOAKES, V. Edward Lear—the life of a wanderer. 1968.

PALMER, A. H. The life of Joseph Wolf. 1895.

Proceedings of the Linnean Society of London 1855–6 (i), pp. xlix–liii Obit. of W. Swainson.

Proceedings of the Royal Society 1881–2, 33, pp. xvii–xix Sclater, P. L. Obit of J. Gould.

READE, B. Edward Lear's parrots. 1949.

SAWYER, F. C. A short history of the libraries and list of the MSS and original drawings in the British Museum (Natural History) Bulletin of B. M. (N.H.) Historical vol. 4. no. 2. 1971.

Scottish Naturalist 1936 Jan/Feb. pp. 2–7 Obit. of A. Thorburn by H. S. Gladstone.

SHARPE, R. B. An analytical index to the works of the late John Gould. 1893.

SWAINSON, W. Taxidermy, with the biographies of zoologists and notices of their works (includes his autobiography). 1840.

WATERHOUSE, F. H. Dates of publication of some of the zoological works of Gould. 1885. (with a biog. sketch).

Who Was Who 1941–50, p. 413 W. F. Frohawk.

WILLIAMS, T. I. A biographical dictionary of scientists. 1969.

WOLLASTON, A. F. R. Life of Alfred Newton. 1921.

WOOD, C. S. An introduction to the literature of vertebrate zoology based chiefly on the titles in the Blacker library of zoology, the Emma Shearer Wood library of ornithology, the Bibliotheca Osleriana and other libraries of the McGill University, Montreal. 1931.

ZIMMER, J. T. Catalogue of the Edward E. Ayer ornithological library. Field Museum, Chicago. 2 vols. 1926.

Zoologist 3rd series 1881, V, pp. 109–115 Harting, J. E. Obit. of J. Gould.

Natural history booksellers, whose catalogues contain much valuable information besides offering for sale the titles discussed in this book:

David Evans, Segry Lawn, Frogham, Fordingbridge, Hampshire.

Bernard Quaritch Ltd., 5–8 Lower John Street, Golden Square, London W1R 4AU.

Wheldon & Wesley Ltd., Lytton Lodge, Codicote, Hitchin, Herts.

NAME INDEX